Praise for

"This is an essential read for any HS parent about to embark on the college search. As one of those parents the concept of a Gap year opens up my thinking about whether HS directly to College is really the best move for my child. I had never really considered the concept but the supporting data that was provided really helped me to see the value."
—Tim Pierce, parent, former higher ed professional and businessman

"Informative, well written, engaging, and super helpful in laying out useful information and concrete steps that the reader can take to figure out what it is best for their learner."
—Karen Goddin, parent and international affairs professional

"School has increasingly become something to endure rather than a place to learn, grow, and develop. What you have shared is so much more than gap years and options other than college, it is a source of inspiration and hope."
—Don Garner, parent, former teacher and learning development specialist."

"I am a parent of a sophomore soon to be junior and it will be the first time I have ever navigated the college system as a parent. It was an excellent introduction to navigating college testing, applications, tuition, scholarship, and administration communication issues before and after taking a gap year and I appreciated the pearls shared."
—Stephanie Farrell, parent and naturopathic physician

"I loved having the recommended action items throughout the book! I also feel that the book really takes on the full picture of considering and experiencing a gap year - the full family impact - and the full experience for the learner."
—Christy Robb, parent and HR professional

"I am grateful for the questions at the end of each chapter. They invited me in to do some reflecting on my own and I know will be useful as we head toward the postsecondary journey with our kids."
—Kristin Brennan Shapiro, parent, kindergarten teacher and former college affordability advisor

Am I Too Late?

Published by
Funk & Myers, Inc.
www.funkandmyers.com

Technical Editor: Mike Myers
Contribution by: Mackenzie Myers

ISBN 978-1-7373145-1-6

Am I Too Late?

A mother's reflection on her son's gap year and how it prepared him for an uncertain world

Cindy Funk & Jim Bellar

This book is dedicated to all the parents who see beyond the confines of traditional education and seek experiences for their students that will prepare them for an exciting, if uncertain, world.

Contents

Introduction
An Uncertain World

One is never afraid of the unknown; one is afraid of the known coming to an end.

— Krishnamurti

Do you remember where you were on September 11th, 2001, when you first learned about the terrorists' attack on the US?

I do. I was driving to work checking in with one of my teammates by phone. He interrupted my update and told me to turn around and go home. "There has been a terrorist attack on New York City and the Pentagon!"

Ten minutes later, I watched the news on television in disbelief and horror as the media reported on two planes flying directly into the Twin Towers in New York City. Soon after that came news of a plane hitting the Pentagon in Washington, D.C. I could not believe what was happening before my eyes and the horrific nature of the attacks!

My first reaction to the news was fear. My brother-in-law Ross worked at the Pentagon and my sister Melodie often traveled to New York City from Connecticut for work. I was afraid that one of them might have been hurt. Worried about my family's safety, I felt compelled to pick up my two sons, Mackenzie and Stuart, from day care and hold them close. I needed to make sure that they were "ok."

I also remember experiencing deep sorrow, for I knew that the world was forever changed that day. My sons, ages two and four at the time, would grow up in a world vastly different from the one I grew up in. They would need to learn to navigate in a world of uncertainty and a place that was no longer "safe."

This is a short list of events that have occurred during my oldest son's lifetime: Columbine High School, 9/11, Iraq War, Afghanistan War, 2008 financial crisis, Hurricane Katrina, BP oil spill, Sandy Hook, Las Vegas, Parkland High School, Me Too Movement, United States Gymnastics Team sex abuse scandal, global climate change and catastrophic weather changes, George Floyd, and now a global pandemic. It is a reality that is shared by most young adults in the US, and the impact has been significant.

When COVID-19 hit, I asked my sons and students I worked with at Portland State University about how they were feeling and what they were thinking about the disruption to their education and lives. Colleges and universities across the country had closed and moved classes online for the rest of the spring semester, because it was no longer safe for them to be open. I was struck by their response—a sense of fatalism. It was almost one of resignation. This crisis was yet again another thing that was out of their control.

You would think that the amount of chaos today's young adults have experienced would have developed in them a high degree of adaptability and resilience. Yet this is not the case. In fact, it is quite the opposite.

As parents, we have sought to protect our children and often coddled them to keep them safe, not wanting them to struggle. This has led many of our young adults to be unwilling to take risks because they don't want to fail. They also don't want to disappoint us, which results in a high degree of stress and anxiety about their future and place in the world. Working in higher education at both private and public institutions over the past ten years, I have seen an increasing fragility in students. This has impacted their ability to launch into adulthood effectively.

One of the first questions I am often asked when I meet with anxious first-year students in my work in career services is: "Am I too late?" They (or their parents) think they have missed out on something, an internship perhaps, that will put them behind in the race to be successful and that time cannot be regained. I can feel the stress and anxiety coming across the table.

There is an overwhelming sense for these students that they are already behind their peers in having a plan for after they graduate. The pressure to compete which began early in life, continues into college. It is alarming to see the frenetic pace in which students engage in their college experience, which often leads to binge drinking, stress, burnout, fear of failure, and lack of focus. Few can get off the treadmill that began in elementary school. They have been conditioned to be busy from a young age by well-meaning parents.

To blame parents would be easy, but the issue is more complex than that. The pressure students face today is baked into a system of individual desires:

(1) the desire of parents for their children to be successful, which means providing the "best" education for them; (2) the desire of students to please their parents, which may mean taking traditional paths and avoiding risks; (3) the desire of high school college counselors for their students to attend the "best" schools; and (4) the desire of college admissions counselors to admit the "best" students while keeping their application/admittance ratio low.

If a student makes it through this gauntlet of desires and is admitted to the "best" school—the pressure is on for four years to make good grades and not drop out.

Personally, I know that I have made mistakes over the years as I navigated parenting my oldest son Mackenzie. From the beginning, however, I have had a vision for what success would look like for him when he is grown. He would be happy, love learning, and using his gifts to make a positive impact on the world.

So how does one go about raising a holistic individual who will become a contributing member of society? How do you raise a child to adulthood who can handle the uncertainty and ambiguity that are the result of constant change, events leading to chaos, and unexpected crises? These thoughts are particularly relevant in a world where COVID-19 has impacted how we live and work.

I don't have the answers but I have often wondered, "What it would take to create an education system that prepares students for constant change? One that helps students develop core competencies that will help them be successful in work and life, and one where they can learn how to pivot when plans don't work out." Included in the list of core competencies would be adaptability and resiliency, and the ability to understand and act with compassion, engage in civil discourse, and share the responsibility of building communities which include work that is equitable.

Thirty-five years ago, as part of my graduate studies at the University of Kansas, I read *A Nation At Risk,* which highlighted the challenges of education and issued a call to action.[1] Since its publication, we have made little progress. Today's K-12 and higher education systems are failing many students, and have increasingly resulted in widening the socio-economic and racial divide. Additionally, we now have a crisis in the number of students who arrive at college campuses with significant mental health issues and emotional well-being challenges.

I offer a unique perspective on the challenges of today's high school and college students as my work over nine years at Vanderbilt University coincided with Mackenzie's adolescence and his transition to emerging adulthood. I could see that he was on an education treadmill. He had been going through the motions of "doing" high school for four years and had all the evidence of burnout. He was unable to break free from the constraints that his education had created. School (the structure and system of delivering education) had squashed his curiosity and joy of learning.

Like the students I was working with at Vanderbilt, I could see him becoming one of the herd, going along with the rest of his peers, not able to see a different path.

I wondered, "What would it take to change his trajectory? Was I too late to help him make a shift? What would happen if he took a year off before starting college? Would it make a difference in helping him launch if he took time to 'breathe'? Or, would he be at a disadvantage when he started college? What would happen if he took a gap year? Would he decide not to go back to school? What would it cost—financially, emotionally, personally?"

This book chronicles my experience in supporting Mackenzie's decision to take time away to engage in his own learning journey, and my observations on the transformation that occurred as a result. The value and benefits of delaying college are clearly illustrated. The book also illuminates challenges that parents and students face as they navigate the high school to college transition.

I am joined in this endeavor by Jim Bellar, my collaborator and co-writer, who provides important background information and research on critical topics related to the subject matter of this book. Jim's perspective is informed by 30 plus years of workforce development in both government and educational settings as well as his own alternative journey after high school. He is a higher education career services professional and career coaching expert who, like me, has worked with individuals from high school dropouts to business executives.

Opinions expressed in this book are based on our collective experience and knowledge gained from working in the "trenches" of higher education guiding students from a range of different backgrounds including first generation college students in their transition to the workplace. Increasingly we have become concerned about the number of students who are not equipped to succeed in an increasingly complex and uncertain world.

We cannot share Mackenzie's story without providing the context of the high school to college transition process, pressures facing students today, and current higher education concerns including admissions and costs. If you are a parent new to the high school to college transition or young adolescent to emerging adult transition, you may find Part I *The Challenge* extremely helpful. We provide information that establishes the economics as well as dispel a few of the myths related to higher education.

If you are eager to read about Mackenzie's learning journey after high school, feel free to jump to Part II *The Journey*.

We have included questions and action steps at the end of each chapter in both Part I and II that, hopefully, will stimulate conversation between you and your young adult (e.g. what does success look like for each of you —does it involve a four-year degree or something different?)

An important caveat about this book; I recognize that not everyone has access to the type of networks and family support reflected in Mackenzie's story. I do believe that this book is relevant for anyone who is interested in considering alternatives to traditional learning, regardless of resources and income. Options for designing a learning journey (aka gap year) are unlimited and can be done at a fraction of the cost of college tuition.

By sharing my story, my hope is that you will understand there is nothing to fear by supporting and encouraging your child to immerse themselves in living and learning outside a classroom. You can make a difference by helping your young adult develop resiliency and be better equipped to deal with today's uncertainty. More than ever, with the current challenges of COVID-19 and its impact on schools, it's not too late to think about "education" and "learning" in a different way.

I once had a middle school principal say to me, "Don't let school get in the way of learning." It was in response to whether my son should accept the invitation from his aunt to experience the Galapagos Islands, which meant missing school for two weeks. You can guess what we decided.

My message to you in this book is: Don't let school get in the way of learning.

Part I

The Challenge

Am I Too Late?

Chapter 1

What Keeps You Up at Night?

Our care of the child should be governed, not by the desire to make him learn things, but by the endeavor always to keep burning within him that light which is called intelligence.

—Maria Montessori

I lost my son.

I can't put my finger on when it happened or what was the trigger, but by the time he reached high school, the little boy who was curious about the world and eager to learn, disengaged. He studied just enough to get good grades and exerted just enough effort so most of his teachers would not suspect that he was underachieving.

I asked myself, what led to this disengagement? Could it be our parenting? Boredom? Depression? Lack of Confidence? Gifted tendency toward perfectionism? What was the reason?

It was not as if the school he attended was an underperforming school. It was just the opposite. Mackenzie attended University School of Nashville (USN), known as one of the best independent schools in the US, whose graduates were admitted to many of the most highly ranked public and private colleges and universities across the country and abroad.

I wondered if we had made a misstep along the way regarding his education. My husband, Mike, and I had chosen to send Mackenzie to USN because of its reputation and focus on college preparation, but at what cost? I felt that we were all on this college-bound train and incapable of jumping off.

"What would it take for him to be happy, content, curious, and thriving?" I wondered.

Dancing with baby

When Mackenzie was born, I had the usual fears of being a "good" Mom. He was my first child and I was committed to learning and being the best parent I could be. To assist with his care, I was fortunate to have access to quality child care through my employer, Colorado College. This is not always the case with working parents. It was a relief to know that he was well cared for while I worked to earn a living.

One evening, after a long day at the office, I arrived to pick Mackenzie up from the daycare center. It was calming to see Helen, a former nurse, in the infant room. She was amazing with infants. On this particular evening, as we were visiting about his day, she gave me some sage advice.

"Just when you think you have figured it out, that you 'got this parent thing down,' he will change and transition into a new stage. And you will have to figure it out all over again, often on the fly, how best to support his development in this new phase. You will continue this dance throughout his life."

Helen called it "Dancing with Baby."

Dancing with baby sounds joyful. It is a beautiful description of what we parents do, as we strive to do what is best for our child, from when they are an infant to when they are an adult. Yet along with the joy, comes fear. And these fears keep us up at night.

There's plenty to worry about when you're a parent

We worry about our child's health and how we are going to pay for health care. We worry about finding and paying for quality childcare. We worry about our child's education and how we are going to pay for college in the future. We worry about our child being bullied for the first time. We worry about our child's safety when there is news of another mass shooting at a school. We worry about our child struggling to meet key developmental milestones. We worry about our child entering early adolescence.

High school years bring additional fears. We worry about our adolescent experimenting with drugs and alcohol and driving a car with the distraction of cell phones. We worry about our adolescent as they begin the transition to becoming an adult. We worry about the impact of the pandemic on our young adult's education and how it will impact college choices and experiences. We worry about our young adult's safety when engaging in protests for social justice and the potential for bodily harm when they cease being peaceful.

Ultimately, we just want our young adult to be happy and successful. What that may mean for us may be perceived differently by our child. We also want them to be "safe."

Parenting is a never-ending responsibility. And the costs of raising a child from infancy to adulthood is not insignificant, both personally and financially. According to the USDA, the average costs of raising one child to the age of 18 is approximately $233,610.[2] Note that this staggering figure does not include private school education or college costs.

Are we that different from our parents?

I often wonder how my parents did it. How they raised five children on a teacher's salary. My Dad taught instrumental and choral music for over 40 years. My mother, who had earned her Associates Degree, often worked as a substitute teacher, raised a large garden to help with food costs, and did a number of other odd jobs including running a nut house with my aunt to earn income. (In case you are wondering, the nut house was not an asylum, but a place that processed whole walnuts and pecans to remove their skins and shells). Socio-economically, we lived just above the poverty level, but I never felt poor because my parents worked hard to make us feel that money was not everything.

What was important, however, was getting an education. My parents believed in education and wanted all of us to attend college. I never felt they pressured me to go; rather, I wanted to go. I was eager to learn and thought that by getting a degree I would be successful in life.

And it did make a difference. After earning my undergraduate degree from the University of Kansas in Communication Studies, I continued my studies and completed a Masters degree in Higher Education Policy and Administration.

My degrees have afforded me the opportunity to work in higher education over the past 35 years at different types of institutions including Colorado College (a small private liberal arts college), Vanderbilt University (a medium-size private university), and Portland State University (a large public institution). From my experience, both personal and professional, I understand the value that a college degree can provide an individual. I also understand higher education's challenges and have twice chosen to pursue work outside academia.

There is no question to me that education is important; but what has increasingly become more apparent is the need for individuals to embrace lifelong learning as necessary to their success. Change is happening at an increasingly exponential rate and adapting will require new skills and knowledge acquisition. Earning a college degree does not reflect the end to one's education / learning journey but can play an important part in an individual's life and overall success.

The best education

While traveling to Boston as part of conducting interviews for this book, I met Diana whose story clearly illustrates the importance we place on education for our children, often equating it with success. Diana was flying from Oakland to Boston to visit her 30-year-old son, his wife, and their 18-month-old child. The couple had relocated to the Boston area from Oakland a few months before and Diana was eager to see them, especially her grandson.

During our conversation, I learned that Diana and her husband had recently retired from successful careers working for the US government. Neither one had completed college and had always desired that their son attend college after high school. They felt that a college degree would provide him opportunities that they had not had access to. When their son informed them of his decision to join the Marines after high school, they were proud of his decision, but were somewhat disappointed that he had chosen this path. Diana had held on to the hope that he would use the GI bill to get his college degree when he separated from the military. Again, she was disappointed when he chose to pursue full-time employment instead of enrolling in college after he completed his military service. At the time of our conversation, Diana's son was working as a heavy equipment salesman and was enjoying much success, professionally and financially. His wife, who had a college degree, coached figure skating and was having success building her business in Massachusetts.

What intrigued me the most about her son's story was the primary reason for the couple's move from Oakland to Boston was their desire for their son to be able to attend one of the "best" public schools in a neighborhood they could afford to live in. Unbelievable! These parents were already thinking about what would be the "best" school for their son and he was not quite two years old!

According to Diana, the couple began looking into education options in the Oakland area when their son was about a year old. What they found was discouraging. The reputation of the public schools for which they were zoned were not favorable. Walnut Creek public schools, known to be some of the best in California, were not an option as they lived two miles beyond the district line and housing was not affordable for them if they were to move to live in this district. The best options they found were parochial and private schools which they could not afford at $17,000/ year. The couple decided to sell their home and make the move to the Boston area because their research found that Massachusetts public schools had a national reputation for being strong academically.

Their decision is not an unusual one. When Mike and I relocated to Tennessee from Colorado, one of the key factors we were looking for in a house to rent in Nashville was that it be located in a neighborhood where the public elementary and secondary schools had a good reputation. Of course, it is not always possible to afford housing where education opportunities are deemed the best, as Diana's son and daughter-in-law realized.

What struck me the most about the couple's decision to move was the lengths that they were willing to take to give their child a better life. I wondered, though, if their preoccupation with having their son get the "best" education might be setting the stage for a childhood and adolescence during which he felt pressured to attend the "best school" because that would define his success in life. He wouldn't want to disappoint them knowing that they had made significant sacrifices for him by moving from California to re-establish their lives in Massachusetts, finding work, new home, etc.

In reflecting on Diana's story, it was hauntingly familiar.

When Mackenzie was ready to begin school, I wanted him to receive the best education we could afford. At the time, public schools in Colorado were ranked 48th out of 50 states in quality of education. Mike and I made the decision to invest in his learning and enrolled him in a Montessori school for pre-school and kindergarten.

It was quite by accident that I learned about Montessori education. I was having a conversation with a friend of a friend while we watched our children playing in the McDonald's play area one afternoon. She mentioned that she had children attending a Montessori school in Colorado Springs. When I heard about the hands-on nature of the Montessori curriculum where learning was self-led and self-paced, I was intrigued. I thought it would be a good fit for Mackenzie. And it was. He thrived. By the end of first grade, he was reading far above his grade level —books like J.R.R. Tolkien's *Lord of the Rings* series and the Harry Potter series. He loved painting, math, and science.

If you are unfamiliar with the Montessori education method like I was, let me share a description provided by American Montessori Society which provides insight into the foundation for Mackenzie's approach to learning early on.

"Within the community of a multi-age classroom—designed to create natural opportunities for independence, citizenship, and accountability— children embrace multi-sensory learning and passionate inquiry. Individual students follow their own curiosity at their own pace, taking the time they need to fully understand each concept and meet individualized learning goals. Given the freedom and support to question, probe deeply, and make connections, Montessori students grow up to be confident, enthusiastic, and self-directed learners and citizens, accountable to both themselves and their community."[3]

What parent would not want this for their child?

Seeking to nurture his curiosity, Mike and I continued to invest in his education by enrolling him in private Montessori schools. With the exception of one-year at a public Montessori elementary school in Colorado Springs that we helped to establish, and which he was the first cohort, Mackenzie completed his primary school years enrolled at small private Montessori schools in Colorado and Florida. He was happy, engaged in learning, and found joy in a number of activities.

The challenge for us was finding the funds to cover private school tuition during his early years. To assist with the costs, we sought financial aid from the schools. We were always grateful when Mackenzie received tuition assistance and scholarships offered by the Montessori schools for him to attend.

As he moved into elementary, middle, and high school, always at the forefront of our thinking was the importance of education to his success. When he began to look at post-secondary options, we were like thousands of other parents in the US. We only wanted what was best for Mackenzie, the best school, the best program of study, the best professors, the best extracurricular activities. Both of us worked in higher education at the time and thought we had a unique perspective. Year after year, we got to witness firsthand, young adults coming to campus, leaving the security of the nest, growing up and graduating to become contributing members of society—a rite of passage that we wanted for our son. One that we had experienced ourselves.

But at the end of the day, we were just like many parents, full of doubt, wondering if we were doing the right thing. College is the second costliest expense after a home mortgage, and with that comes more scrutiny from parents and students.

Mackenzie at Montessori school

When Mike and I were considering ways to pay for college, there was one eye-popping statistic that stopped us in our tracks: over a 17-year period, the change in college tuition compared to other basic living expenses, including medical and hospital costs, had increased the most—a whopping 357% increase. Take a look at the graph below and you might see why we had cause for worry.

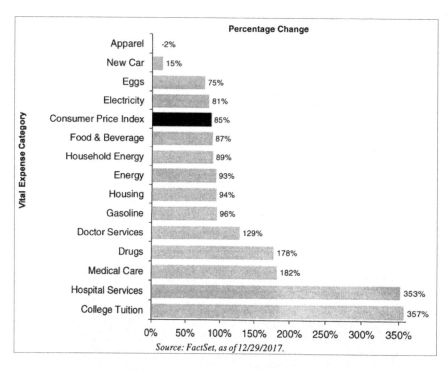

Change in college tuition from December 1990 - December 2017 compared with other costs

And this number has continued to increase since 2017.

If you are a parent seeing this statistic for the first time, I am guessing you might be asking yourself "How can I afford sending my child to college?"

And what if you have more than one child?

Paying for college is just one of a few questions that you might find yourself pondering in the middle of the night when you can't sleep. I've taken the liberty of sharing a few others that contributed to my fears followed by answers designed to inform and challenge your thinking.

What is the purpose of college?

No easy answer here. Ask any high school student, parent, academic, graduate, alumnus, or board member and you may get very different answers. "To get a good job." "To have a broader understanding of the world." "To prepare students to be global citizens."

The answer is YES!

There are at least two popular camps today when it comes to deciding the purpose of college.

The problem is that our national narrative about "college" has created a decidedly false dichotomy between the two primarily professed purposes of college. There is the camp that says college is about preparing a person for work—to help them get a good or better job. In fact, this is by far the most commonly cited reason for why Americans value higher education—to get a good job. The other camp says college is about more broadly preparing a person for success in life—to be an engaged and enlightened citizen capable of thinking critically and communicating clearly, ultimately able to thrive in their well-being. Make no mistake, many of us see the purpose of college as both a job-driven and a life-driven purpose. But our dialogue is horribly stuck in the muck of an either/or debate on these two fronts.[4]

How much will college cost and can I afford it?

It is hard to say. Factors of affordability depend on a number of things—planning, budgeting, saving, choice of college, and let's not forget the financial aid award which often includes student and parent loans.

When loans are offered as part of the overall aid package by a college or university, there is a lack of transparency in actual costs of the loans. Federal Direct Unsubsidized Loans and Federal Direct Parent Plus Loans that students and parents often utilize to pay for college must be paid back and begin immediately accruing interest.[5] This expense is never reflected in the total cost for students to attend college. The interest on federal unsubsidized loans ranges from 4.5% to over 7% depending on the loan. Interest on private loans is often much higher.

The average student debt (depending on which source you believe) is more than $32,000 a year, and parents and grandparents are increasingly on the hook for tuition. The latest student loan debt statistics in 2020 reveal that student borrowers across all demographics and age groups owe nearly $1.6 trillion.[6] Student loan debt is now the second highest consumer debt category—behind mortgage debt—and is higher than both credit cards and auto loans. Due to the increasing costs of college tuition, parents and grandparents have borrowed to help pay for college through Parent PLUS loans and parent loans offered through private lenders. Parents now owe nearly $100 billion for student loans![7]

The key takeaway here; it is important for you to know what you are getting into if you are choosing to take out loans to help pay for your student's education.

What if my student chooses the wrong major?

There is significant debate and commentary about what majors students "should" major in and those to avoid if they want to get a job. Many argue that majoring in one of the STEM fields will help a student get a job after graduation where as a liberal arts degree will not.

For years, the debate on the value of the liberal arts degree has received a lot of attention with different stakeholders weighing in. As someone who majored in the liberal arts, I understand the value of this type of degree. However, I also recognize the challenges liberal arts graduates often face in articulating what they have learned from their education and connecting it to career opportunities immediately following college.

As you begin to have conversations with your young adult about what major they might want to choose in college, know that when they get to campus, that it is not a scientific process. Decisions may be influenced by a variety of stakeholders including you as parents, teachers, and friends, or a happenstance meeting or whim.

According to a Forbes article, "career" and "passion" are two words that pop up a lot in the conversation.[8] "A student's desire for a major that is in line with their interests can be categorized as their passion. Parents and schools, meanwhile, typically advise students to find a degree that will lead to a solid career. These potentially opposing factors are the main components of a student's search criteria. Another detail worth pointing out is how college majors fall on either 'passion' or 'career' and rarely overlap. For example, the study showed that many students view Medicine, Accounting and Marketing as a 'career', while English and Fine Arts are considered 'passion' majors."

It's little wonder that 30% of students change majors at least one time while in college, and one in ten change majors two or more times.[9] I confess, I changed majors three times during my first two years at KU. I started as a Theatre Voice major in the College of Fine Arts, switched to Music Education offered through the College of Education, and finally landed in the College of Arts and Science majoring in Communication Studies. My experience is still a fairly typical journey taken by college students today. The difference, however, is today's college costs make switching majors an expensive experiment in finding the right major.

Due diligence is always a good idea, but trying to map a process and predict an outcome with so many variables (school, major, your student's physical and mental health, job market, etc.) can be an exercise in frustration where you and your student may get equally stressed over something you can't control.

Some other stats to consider: A recent survey found that 36% of graduates would choose a different major if they could. Another survey found that only 27% of college graduates work in a field related to their major.[10]

There is no magic major that guarantees your student will be successful in the job market. Overstock CEO Patrick Bryne majored in Philosophy and Asian Studies and Chipotle CEO Steve Ells majored in history.[11]

"Not surprisingly, the typical path is more of a swirl than a straight line. The results don't look like neat cohorts entering a few high-profile careers with perfect intentionality," says Rob Sentz, Chief Innovation Officer at the nonprofit Emsi and co-author of a report on career pathways of college graduates based on majors. "Instead, we see something that looks much more like 'real' people moving in the market based on a complex web of factors, changing over time, finding their way and adapting as they go."[12]

What if my student drops out of school?

A Washington Post article by Jeff Selingo says that fewer than 40% of first-time students graduate in four years. More than half who start community colleges drop out within six years. "Basically, wealthy students graduated, and low-income students did not. Children from families earning more than $90,000 have a 1-in-2 chance of getting a bachelor's degree by 24. That falls to a 1 in 17 chance for families earning under $35,000."[13]

Of course, dropping out of school does not necessarily mean students will not be successful. Apple co-founder Steve Jobs, Facebook CEO Mark Zuckerburg and Microsoft co-founder Bill Gates are just a few individuals who dropped out of college and have garnered much success in the tech world. It is important to note, however, that these individuals had access to resources that not everyone has and family and networks that supported them.

What happens if my student graduates with no job?

For a large number of graduates, employment is not one of the immediate outcomes of their getting a degree.

According to Consumer Affairs, it takes the average college graduate 7.4 months to find a job after graduation. Couple that with the fact that 40% of graduates enter jobs that do not require a degree.[14]

A number of factors play a role in how successful a graduate will be in securing a job including their academic major, internship experience, access to opportunities through their family and school networks, etc. For instance, liberal arts graduates usually take longer than other majors to get a job.

In over 20 plus years collecting outcomes data at institutions known for their focus on liberal arts, I have found that liberal arts graduates often don't land their first "professional" role until about 18 months after graduation. That is why a number of liberal arts graduates end up pursuing graduate studies as their default next step. They are not sure what they want to do so graduate school delays their career decision a little longer. Of course, there are exceptions. For specific industries and certain professional work (one being higher education) it is important to have a graduate degree to be competitive.

Please know that I am not saying that liberal arts graduates will never get a job. It just may take them a little longer to find work that fits.

What's more concerning for me is that employers are finding that many graduates are not prepared for starting a professional job which leads to their unemployment or underemployment.[15]

Having a degree doesn't guarantee a job.

Will my student live with me forever?

Depending on your relationship with your emerging adult, this question may or may not strike fear in you. For me, I enjoy spending time with Mackenzie. Now that we are past the adolescent phase of his life, I have fun enjoying the person he has become as an adult. (Though, my grocery bill is a lot less when he is not around!) I recognize, however, that it is better for him to feel that he has the independence of living on his own. It establishes a healthier parent/child relationship.

Many young adults do not have the choice of whether to live with their parents when they graduate. Even pre-pandemic, a Forbes article estimated that 50% of Millennials plan to move back home with their parents after college and 31% plan to move back for at least two years.[16]

There are many reasons for this, including the high cost of housing, the economy, healthcare, and student debt.

And with the introduction of a global pandemic, it's hard to imagine this trend will go away any time soon. According to a recent Pew Research Center analysis of Current Population Survey data, about 52% of young Americans ages 18 to 29 are now living with at least one of their parents. This number surpassed the previous record of 48%, which was set in 1940 during the Great Depression.[17]

The good news: the pandemic has brought many families closer together and social norms are changing about generations of families living together.

What You Can Do

1. Ask yourself what success would look like for your young adult and share this with them.
2. Engage your young adult in a conversation about the purpose of college and expectations.
3. Work with your young adult in developing a spreadsheet with projected costs for four to five years of college—include interest on loans if this will be part of funding college.

Notes

Am I Too Late?

Chapter 2
Coloring Outside the Lines

The truth is rarely pure and never simple.
—Oscar Wilde, The Importance of Being Earnest

"I can't do it,"Mackenzie sobbed, "I can't color in the lines!"

Mike and I looked in consternation at our 6-year-old son sitting in tears beside us. It was an unusual sight for our normally easy-going child. He had just finished his first week of first grade at Gateway Elementary, a public school in Woodland Park, CO.

Concerned, I asked him, "What do you mean, you can't color in the lines?"

With a voice choked by tears, he replied, "At school, I can't color in the lines. I keep running out of time."

I asked, "What are you coloring?" He replied, "a balloon picture. I have to color inside the lines before the teacher says 'stop.'" He sobbed harder.

I was appalled. Mackenzie was being asked to color a picture within a set time. The only reason that I could think of was to prepare him for timed tests. This was the first week of first grade!

From my work as a career counselor helping undergraduate and graduate students majoring in education at Regis University, I had heard that public schools had changed significantly since the passage of "No Child Left Behind" legislation. The focus on standardized testing was often detrimental to the learning process. Many education majors were considering not teaching once they completed their degree requirements, because the focus on standardized tests did not allow for flexibility and freedom in the classroom. I had not personally experienced the impact on the learning environment until I saw firsthand my son's response to the testing simulation.

The following week when I spoke to Mackenzie's teacher about his weekend outburst, she confirmed that this exercise was part of preparing students to take standardized tests.

What would this mean for him long term? I wondered.

The system versus the individual

There are exceptions, but education, including higher education, is built on a foundation of repetition, predictability, and assumptions that the system works for all students. The process is sometimes unkind to students (and parents) who "color outside the lines."

Children born with a learning difference like our youngest son, Stuart, particularly struggle. Parents have to continually advocate for their special needs child, even through young adulthood, as they navigate systems set up for neurotypical learners.

To help our child negotiate increasingly complex systems that are inherent in today's schools, we often find ourselves having to be navigators, explorers, detectives, and data scientists. Some of us seek answers and are drawn to books like this one.

When it comes to helping our student with the college search process, it can be particularly overwhelming. There are tons of options, and slick marketing abounds from most institutions. When Mackenzie was in high school, the amount of information he received through print and on-line communications from schools vying for his attention (and his application) was staggering. I would often read the glossy materials he received from the different admissions offices because I was curious as to what they shared regarding outcomes of a degree from their particular school.

With all the "noise" that this creates, it is easy to get caught up in the messaging about what attending college means and what a college degree will do for graduates. It is implied that graduates will know certain things about life and understand how the world works. Unfortunately, over the years, myths have formed as a result of all the hyperbole.

One of the challenges in choosing a school—any school—is that there are no guarantees. College is not a turnkey experience like buying a new house where everything is expected to be in working order once the contract is signed. If you buy a new car and the engine blows up at 29,000 miles, there is a warranty that covers this. Later on, if the windshield on that car proves to be defective, a recall may be issued and that part replaced for free. In higher ed, there is no contract. If a student graduates without a job, picks the wrong major, didn't get an internship —the onus is on the student, not the institution, and the debt rarely goes away.

As you and your young adult explore options that are primarily focused on a four-year post-secondary degree, here are a few myths to consider:

Myth #1: Someone will help my student decide on the best major or degree to pursue

At many colleges and universities, faculty are responsible for advising students. However, the quality and effectiveness of academic advising done by faculty varies. This has led a number of institutions to employ academic advisors who help students stay on track to complete their degrees. Unfortunately, academic advisors are not career advisors. These advisors understand requirements for the degree but have limited knowledge on how majors align with careers and are often unfamiliar with careers outside their fields of expertise.

If students utilize their campus career center, they can find assistance with choosing a major aligned with career interests, but most don't engage with this office. Rather, they choose to turn to faculty members, parents, relatives, or peers for help with choosing a major and getting career guidance.

When I was at Vanderbilt University, our office led a focus group for engineering students on their career planning needs. Overwhelmingly, students said that they would go to their faculty advisor when they had questions about their academic major or needed career advice. The next person they would seek advice from was a peer or fellow student, followed by a relative such as a parent or an older sibling. Not one student said they would use the campus career center.

These findings were similar to what I found years before when I conducted research for my masters thesis. I surveyed students entering the University of Kansas and their faculty advisors about their perceptions of academic advising. There was a clear difference in what students perceived the role of faculty would be in helping them choose a major and what faculty view of their role was in this process. Students saw faculty as the primary source for help with choosing a major and faculty did not.

Myth #2: College will help my student mature and acquire important life skills

There are less costly ways to gain maturity and there is no guarantee, especially at universities where students are required to live on campus, that students will grow up.

I am not saying that maturation does not occur for college students, but the difference in maturity of someone who has taken a year off before college is markedly different than that of an entering first-year student who has come straight from high school.

Because we have coddled many of our young adults, they arrive at college lacking maturity. Higher education, in turn, has responded by creating an entire profession of student affairs administrators (yes, I was one of them) whose sole purpose is to help students develop. Despite our best intentions, the result has often been to continue coddling students as they go through their undergraduate experience. Thus, the pace of traditional students' maturation is significantly slower than students who have been independent prior to attending college.

When I went to college, I was fortunate to secure a housing spot in Sellards Scholarship Hall, one of eight residential housing units at the University of Kansas at the time, where I lived in a house with 45 other students (all women) as part of a cooperative living community. It was a truly unique and formative experience for me.

Residents were assigned four to a (small) suite and there was a shared bathroom on each floor. There was also a laundry room in the basement next to the kitchen. It is where I learned how to run a HOBI dishwasher—often used at restaurants.

We each were expected to work a minimum of six hours a week to contribute to the community and maintain the community's physical space—this might include dishwashing duty, bathroom cleaning duty, breakfast cooking, etc. In addition, residents shared common duties such as covering the front desk (after all, we still had to ensure safety) where we would use a buzzer along with a morse code that had been assigned to each resident to alert her when she had a guest or if she had a phone call. To this day, I still remember my call sign: - . --.

I compare this to today's residential halls where students live and learn. The opulence and grandeur of new residence halls on college campuses has been covered by the media, raising questions about why these are necessary. I tend to agree.

In efforts to recruit students, colleges and universities seek to compete with each other by building and providing housing that meets students every need. From providing laundry service to food service, where students can choose items from a hot bar, wood-fired pizza counter, salad bar, ice cream bar, deli counter, pasta bar, etc. Students can live in a single, double, triple, or quadruple suite, often with their own bathroom or one shared with two or three other students.

Housekeeping staff take care of cleaning halls and common spaces. Paid desk and security staff take care of students ensuring their safety. Paid student development professionals take care of students' emotional well-boing. With all of their day-to-day living needs taken care of, it's no wonder today's students are slow to gain independence and lack a sense of accountability for their actions.

Building community requires that students feel accountable to others and their surroundings. On today's campuses, you will often find underpaid housing staff cleaning up after students, not only in their residence halls, but in other campus buildings and outdoor areas.

Why not create living learning communities and residential facilities that are modeled more like what I experienced? It would definitely be less expensive to operate this model. More importantly, students would learn life-lessons critical for launching into the world.

As for other important life skills needed to effectively launch as an adult, few, if any, colleges provide mandatory courses in finance, relationship building, negotiation, and understanding contracts (including student loans).

These skills would be helpful for graduates to learn as they navigate an uncertain world filled with mortgages, car loans, credit cards and salaries that have to be negotiated.

University of Kansas Sellards Scholarship Hall

Myth #3: Someone will get a job for my student

College administrators sometimes market their schools to prospective parents by telling them about their career center's "placement rate" and brand-name employers that recruit on campus. If the goal is for your student to be employed when they graduate; this may sound pretty good.

But according to a 2017 Strada-Gallup College Student Survey, only about 20% of students use career centers. The survey, given to students enrolled across 43 randomly selected colleges and universities, both public and private, revealed that students used career centers for services like resume reviews and taking skills tests, but were less likely to use them for career information or finding jobs. Many centers are understaffed and underfunded and even the ones that have adequate staffing may be in geographic areas where employers do not recruit or where the school may not have strong alumni connections.[18]

If you are encouraging your student to choose a college based on employment opportunities, you should understand the difference between (1) "placement rates" (graduate destinations including employment, graduate school, military, taking time off, etc.) (2) employment rates (number of graduates who actually have jobs) and (3) the number of graduates employed in their fields of study (e.g., music, engineering, education). You, or your student, should ask about the sample size and the period when the survey was conducted to get a true picture of what these numbers mean.

Myth #4: Colleges teach the skills that are in demand by employers

There is a disconnect between skills and experiences the job market demands and what four-year colleges can provide. Part of this gap is due to the length of time it takes for a university program to get up and running after employer feedback is received. Those skills and knowledge may be outdated by then. That's assuming that universities are actively seeking employer feedback to inform their curricular offerings. From my experience working at several institutions, this rarely or never happens. Feedback regarding skills deficits we would receive from employers often fell on deaf ears when we sought to share this information with faculty and college administration.

Jane Oates, a former official in the U.S. Department of Labor during the Obama administration, who is now President of Working Nation, is a strong advocate for work-based learning in schools. She says it's not enough for colleges to be more intentional about including workforce-relevant skills in their degree programs. "Employers have to be doing this simultaneously."[19]

Some companies have eliminated the college degree as a job requirement in order to recruit from a broader base. "When you look at people who don't go to school and make their way in the world, those are exceptional human beings. And we should do everything we can to find those people," said Google's former SVP of People Operations Laszlo Bock.

Maggie Stilwell, Ernst and Young's Managing Partner for Talent, added that "academic qualifications will still be taken into account and indeed remain an important consideration when assessing candidates as a whole, but will no longer act as a barrier to getting a foot in the door."

Myth #5: College will set my student on the right career path

In pre-pandemic America, millennials were changing jobs an average of four times in the first 10 years after graduation. LinkedIn economist, Guy Berger, who analyzed the career trajectories of three million college graduates, declares: "a college degree used to slot you into a 40-year career. Now it's just an entry-level point to your first job." He said graduates are not just changing jobs; "they often change into entirely different industries."[20]

Part of this churn is due to technology advances, which may prompt employers to eliminate positions and search for skills sets that support the current needs of the company. Some say that nearly 40% of US jobs are in occupations that are likely to shrink or be cut by 2030.[21]

Another factor is the changing expectations of the younger generation—a generation that wants to be paid more and advance up the ranks quickly. "Approximately 40 percent of employees who quit in 2017 did so within 12 months of being hired, according to a study based on data from over 34,000 exit interviews analyzed by Work Institute, a workplace research and consulting firm in Franklin, Tennessee. About half of workers who departed in their first year left quickly—within the first 90 days.[22]

Learning can occur anywhere

The impact of the coronavirus and how universities shifted their classes to online learning may change higher education forever. It highlights the reality that "learning" can occur anywhere.

"Education" is not synonymous with "learning." Students educated through the structure of a traditional classroom environment often learn and acquire knowledge. However, how much they retain is the question. The most powerful learning occurs when a student is immersed in an experience followed by reflection.

There is an exciting movement in the K-12 space to revolutionize education through a focus on experiential learning. Dr. Chris Unger co-leads Northeastern University's NExT initiative—a network that is reimagining what high school can look like. If you want to be inspired, I encourage you to checkout his podcasts about innovation in education.[23]

Fun Fact: Almost 40% of students in college today are adult learners (ages 25+), not recent high school graduates.

One particular school featured in his podcasts refers to all their "students" as "learners." I am struck by the difference in how I think about the conversation of education and learning by simply replacing the term "student" with the term "learner." "Student" seems passive and "learner" seems active.

It is not surprising that Northeastern University is part of the conversation of how education can be disrupted. It was one of the first universities to establish a cooperative education program in the US. Northeastern students have the option of completing one or two coops, which are similar to internships, during their four years of studies.

Many universities value experiential learning and offer students the option of gaining this experience through study abroad and internships. Unfortunately, these options are typically not an integral part of a student's academic studies.

Paradigms to shift

Currently, there are numerous discussions about the need for education reform in the US (including higher education) happening at the local, state, regional, and national levels. And not a day goes by where you can't find a news article related to this topic. It reminds me of similar discourse that was occurring while I was doing my graduate work at KU in the 1980s.

From my perspective, little has changed over the past 45 years. Because of the important role that we continue to assign to higher education institutions today in preparing students for life after college, I wanted to touch upon it in this chapter to help you understand what is at stake as you consider post-secondary learning options for your young adult.

Over the last ten years, I have been in a unique position working as a higher education career services professional whose job is to facilitate connections between students and employers to achieve specific outcomes; for students, it's often to secure an internship or full-time job; for employers, it's to hire top talent aligned with their business needs. What I have heard increasingly from employers over the last ten years—at both an elite private institution and a large state university—is that many students lack core competencies needed to be successful in the workplace.

Why is this the case, you may be wondering?

In her groundbreaking book, *The New Education. How to revolutionize the university to prepare students for a world in flux*, author Cathy Davidson provides insight into why today's colleges and universities are failing to prepare students.[24] Her perspective is informed by many years spent as a faculty member and administrator focused on innovation at Duke University and current role directing the Future Initiatives at the City University of New York (CUNY).

An Industrial Age model in the 21st century

At the root of the problem, Davidson suggests, is today's higher education model, invented 150 years ago to prepare young people for the industrial age, is no longer relevant. The model has not adapted to meet the changes brought on by "upheaval" created by transformative technologies including the advent of the Internet. Tuition has soared while universities continue to maintain the status quo—an enduring system of grades, departments, and graduate and professional schools—designed to train students for stable, lifelong work.

"As was the age of industrialization," she writes, "the Internet era has been marked by complex and far-reaching social, political, and economic changes wrought not by steam power and assembly-line mechanization but by digitization and algorithm-based global redistribution of ideas, capital, goods, labor, and services. Modern networked computing changed everyday life and work, and these changes accelerate each year. Even our ideas about what it means to be human and social—a 'self' and a 'society'—fail to encompass the close ties of people who never physically meet, who can interact virtually—as friends, lovers, or trolls—and who may not even be who they say they are. Suddenly, we spend more time online than off, interacting in a world with no centralized publisher, no editor, no broadcaster controlling, filtering, or verifying content; all of our vast power to access and communicate anything at all is available without a pause or a retract button. Everyone has a platform. No professional-managerial class is in charge. No degree required."

Davidson advocates changing the model to one that emphasizes creativity, collaboration, and adaptability along with the opportunity for students to work on multidisciplinary, real-world problems—teaching them not just how to think, but how to learn. "If we can revolutionize our colleges and universities so that we do not reach to the test but rather challenge and empower students, we will do the best possible job helping them to succeed in an uncertain world...The goal of higher education is greater than workforce readiness. It's world readiness."

The good news is that there are a colleges and universities that are beginning to work on new models for higher education. Innovation is happening at community colleges, liberal arts colleges, regional public universities, and massive state universities. I encourage you to consider these institutions if you are helping your young adult identify college options. Depending on their goals, one of these institutions might be a better fit than a more expensive, highly prestigious university.

Don't forget community colleges

As I reflect on our mindset when Mackenzie was in high school, I am not sure why we did not explore community college as another post-secondary option for him besides pursuing a four-year degree. Maybe it was because I never considered this option for myself when I was applying to colleges. It was not something I discussed with my parents which is interesting, since they both attended community college for part of their post-secondary education.

Another reason, I was less familiar with community colleges and what they offered. I also don't recall that attending community college was part of the conversation at Mackenzie's high school—a fact that might be something to reconsider in light of college costs today. Granted, Mike and I had invested significant resources for him to attend a high school that was academically strong and known for preparing its graduates for college. Unknowingly, we became trapped into thinking that his success was defined by him graduating from high school and attending a highly ranked four-year college. Community college was not on our radar.

From my work at Portland State University, I have seen the value of students attending community college before transferring to a four-year university. Approximately two-thirds of PSU students are community college transfers. It is definitely a more affordable option for many students. They can spend two years completing general requirements at a community college for a fraction of the cost they would pay at a four-year school. There are also a number of excellent one and two year career training programs offered through community colleges that don't require a student to get a four-year degree—students can enter the workforce right away.

Of course, the residential campus experience that many of us visualize as essential to college studies for our young adult (and what is highlighted a great deal by popular media) is missing. There is a long-held belief that the residential experience is a necessary part of college as it will help young adults grow up. Though I agree that this experience can be part of students' learning in college, as I suggested earlier in this chapter, I think that today's residential campus experience may not necessarily be developing life skills critical to students' success.

Overseas degrees—cheaper and quicker

Another option that was not on our radar as Mackenzie engaged in the college search process, was the option of earning a degree overseas. It was not until the daughter of a friend of mine decided to pursue her post-secondary studies abroad, that I learned how viable and cost effective this option could be for students. If you and your young adult want to explore post-secondary options abroad, there was one resource that this family discovered that they found particularly helpful, Beyond the States.[25] It is a company offering a "database of 1700+ accredited English-taught programs in continental Europe (not the UK or Ireland)." The Founder of Beyond the States, Jennifer Viemont, has also authored *College Beyond the States. European Schools That Will Change Your Life Without Breaking The Bank*, a helpful book on the subject.[26]

It is important to note that most colleges and universities overseas do not offer a residential experience. Students live on their own, or with roommates, in housing they have arranged and handle all the responsibilities that this entails. What is compelling about earning a degree from another country is that the cost is significantly less and can often be completed in three years.

At the end of the day, it's about preparing your young adult for the world ahead to help them be successful. There are many ways to reach the same objective and it is important to keep an open mindset. I invite you to consider reframing the college experience by exploring alternative two-year, three-year, and four-year options with your young adult. It's okay to color outside the lines! No college can provide all of the experiences and information that your student will need, because we don't know what they will need because of the pace of change. Learning will happen over and over again; a degree is only a starting point.

What You Can Do

1. Sit down with your young adult and tell them about your life:
   - What you wanted to be after high school
   - The career your parents wanted for you
   - How you chose the college or training you attended or why you didn't go to college
   - Who paid for your college and training
   - Why you chose your major(s)
   - What you wanted to do after college
   - Your first job and how you got it—knowledge you used from college—how much money did you make
   - Your work life and how you have changed jobs—are the jobs all different or similar
   - Your favorite courses
   - Your favorite experiences
2. Have your young adult engage in a brainstorming activity with you to discuss alternative ways to reach their goals (e.g., obtain a diploma, live an interesting life, make a lot of money).

Notes

Chapter 3
College Admissions Gone Wild

You are enough. And anyone who tells you otherwise isn't worth your time.

—Dolly Parton

Applying to college is like buying a new car; there are thousands of vehicles on the lot, a variety of features, energy efficiencies, maintenance costs, prices, payment plans, etc. Some are faster and more luxurious. At the end of the day, though, they're all cars, capable of getting the driver down the road.

There are plenty of sales professionals roaming the lot to answer questions and help the consumer determine if a Toyota is better than a Nissan or a Tesla.

College admissions is sales—maybe not the high pressure kind, but there is a feeling that if you don't buy today, you may miss out.

Five Things I Learned About College Admissions

Here are some tidbits that may be helpful for you to know as your student navigates the complicated process of college admissions. Like buying a car, the research done on the front end may save you and your student time and lots of money in the future.

1. Parents have to learn how to play the game

For us, our education in playing the game, began in Mackenzie's freshman year of high school. That's right—freshman year! And yes, I say "our" because it was expected that parents be engaged in the college search process at some level, beginning in the student's 9th grade year.

Since 4th grade, Mike and I had made a financial commitment to enroll Mackenzie at University School of Nashville (USN), an independent K-12 college preparatory school, known for its quality teaching and bright students. It also had a reputation of graduating students who enrolled at many of the top higher education institutions across the US.[27]

With the public high school graduation rate in Nashville hovering around 67%, we sought to provide Mackenzie with the best education possible. Sound familiar?

Each year, when we had to figure a way to pay the tuition bill, we would say to ourselves that this investment in his education would pay off. By sending him to such a "good" school, he would have lots of opportunities

Mackenzie starts University School of Nashville

to attend some of the "best" and "top" colleges and universities in the US —schools with large endowments, who would make financial awards to bright, deserving students, like our son covering all expenses.

Perfect plan, right? Well, definitely a plan. One that did not work out quite like we thought.

But I'm getting ahead of myself. Let's get back to the college search process.

So why did we as parents need to be engaged?

Initially, I did not understand the reason for my involvement, but the more I learned about the college admissions process, the more I realized the importance of my being an informed parent.

What became clear was that the admissions process had changed significantly since I was in high school. I was struck by how challenging the process had become for students and parents to navigate, and this troubled me. College admissions used to be much simpler. At least in my mind, the process had been less complex when I was college age.

My perspective is informed by my own college search process in high school and by my later work in college admissions. When I applied to college, I applied to three state institutions and went to the school that offered me the program of study that I was interested in and gave me the most financial aid. I spent two summers working for the Office of Undergraduate Admissions at the University of Kansas and that experience solidified my interest in pursuing a masters degree in higher education. Fast forward 25-plus years, when I found myself alarmed at the changes that had become part of the college admissions process.

2. The process starts early

When Mackenzie was a 7th grade student, he was encouraged to consider joining Duke TIP—a program that targets talented and gifted students—based on his score on the ERB test (an achievement test utilized by independent schools).[28] It also acts as a feeder program for schools like Duke University. To participate, Mackenzie was encouraged to take one or both standardized tests: the ACT and the SAT.[29] [30] Mind you, the SAT and ACT are typically given during junior and senior years of high school, and he was only in 7th grade!

Mackenzie consulted with USN's academic advisor and decided to take both the ACT and SAT. A number of his other classmates were also taking the tests, so he felt he was not alone. Up to this point in his education, he had enjoyed taking standardized tests and thought they were fun. Taking a couple of Saturdays to take tests was not that big a deal to him and he was not concerned about his scores.

Interestingly enough, Mackenzie achieved a high score on one of the test areas of the ACT and received a Grand Recognition Award at a ceremony hosted by the Duke TIP program.[31] I had no idea what this recognition meant, but, in talking with a colleague of mine at Vanderbilt University who had worked for the Duke TIP program for many years, I discovered that very few students achieved this recognition. She said his score was very high and that we should be very proud of him. Of course, what mother wouldn't be proud when she hears her son is special and smart!

Now that I knew Mackenzie had a particular gift, I wondered how we could nurture this gift. Because that's what parents are supposed to do, right? So I began to research opportunities.

One opportunity would be to enroll him in a Duke TIP summer or weekend enrichment program. However, in looking at the costs for different programs, I realized we could not afford the additional expense. We hoped that by continuing to enroll him at USN, that the education and experiences offered through the school would be enough to develop his gift.

In reflecting on Mackenzie's high school experience, I sometimes wonder what would have happened if we had enrolled Mackenzie in the Duke TIP enrichment programs. What impact would these experiences have had on his development and learning during high school? Would it have made a difference in college admissions?

Freshman Year—information meetings

At USN, experienced college counselors knowledgeable of the college admissions process work with students over four years to prepare them for the college search. Parents are included in this educational process.

Early in Mackenzie's freshman year, we received an invitation to attend a parent information meeting on how USN approached the college counseling process. Being parents of a high school student for the first time, Mike and I both attended the meeting. The room was overflowing with parents eager to get the inside scoop on how they could support their young adult and position them for a successful college search. What amazed me was that our children were only freshmen in high school, yet here we were, already concerned about college planning!

During the meeting, the school's college counselors assured us to not worry. They encouraged us to support our child throughout their high school experience. They asked us to encourage our student to take academic risks and take classes that they would not normally take, make new friends, and engage in activities that would stretch them. They made the case that high school should **not** be focussed on building a resume for the college application but rather a time for our student to find their voice—to learn a lot about themselves as individuals. They strongly encouraged us to step back and not worry about the process. Basically, "take a breath, parents, we got this!"

Sophomore Year—testing introduced

During Mackenzie's sophomore year, there was another parent information meeting where the college counselors shared information on the activities that students would be engaged in over the academic year. One included taking the PSAT test in the spring semester. The PSAT/NMSQT (National Merit Scholarship Qualifying Test) is a practice version of the SAT exam and is used to prepare students to take the SAT test during their junior and senior years. Based on a student's PSAT performance, they could potentially qualify to compete for merit scholarships offered through the National Merit Scholarship Program.[32] This designation is important to colleges and universities and is often taken into consideration in admissions selections and financial aid awards.

The college counselors assured us that the PSAT was helpful practice for taking the SAT. They shared that they had urged students not to be stressed about taking the test; however, a contradictory message was also delivered. The students had been encouraged to complete the practice test so they could be prepared and "perform at the best of their ability." We were asked to remind our student about taking the practice test. Again, I was struck by how early the focus was on college admissions at his school. Mackenzie had two and a-half more years before he graduated, yet, standardized testing for college admissions had already begun!

As you can imagine, despite the messaging from the counselors, students felt pressured to compete with their peers to make a high scored on the PSAT. It was at this point during sophomore year that Mackenzie and a number of his classmates began competing for recognition tied to college admissions and scholarships. Just another thing to add to students' stress levels and anxiety about the college search.

Even more problematic for me was the PSAT set in motion a focus on standardized testing that impacted Mackenzie's last two years of high school.

Junior Year—ACT and SAT strategy

Mackenzie was encouraged to take both the ACT and SAT standardized tests and see which one he performed better on. After taking both tests during his junior year, he found that he had done much better on the ACT, so he decided that he would focus on elevating his score by taking the exam again his senior year.

Mackenzie's approach was not a bad strategy. Selective college admissions officers look at a student's standardized test score and it carries significant weight in admissions decisions. Standardized test scores also impact the type of scholarships that a student receives as part of their financial aid award. Higher scores often equate to merit scholarship awards. State schools, in particular, look at a student's performance on the ACT or SAT along with their high school GPA. The higher the number, the more money a student can receive in student scholarships and financial aid.

What puzzles me most is why SAT and ACT scores have been such big factors in college admissions decisions and financial aid awards. Particularly, when you look at the background and history behind IQ tests which were developed by researchers attached to the eugenics movement. If you are not familiar with eugenics, it is the idea that humans with good qualities should be allowed to breed and pass on those qualities, while humans with bad qualities should be discouraged from having children (or if they had defective qualities, they be sterilized).[33]

Scary when you think that the work of these individuals is part of making college admission decisions!

The inherent inequality of standardized tests has been recognized by colleges and universities for years, but, before the pandemic, most still required test scores to be submitted as part of a student's college application. Many students do not have the kind of preparation for taking these tests that students with financial means have. At USN, a number of students paid for test prep courses, or their parents hired SAT/ACT tutors to help them prepare.

When Mackenzie asked us if we would pay for a tutor his senior year to help him raise his ACT scores, we agreed. Looking back, I realize that our response should have been to say "no." Instead, we got caught up in the madness surrounding the college search process.

Mackenzie's goal was to take the ACT multiple times to achieve a "superscore." He was seeking to raise his math score. Many colleges allow students to list their best test scores on individual sections of the ACT (English, Math, Reading, and Science) when submitting their scores on their application. The school then calculates a "super composite," or superscore, which reflects a student's best result. A superscore is accepted by a number of colleges and universities and can influence the college admissions decision.

Increasingly, I became concerned by what I observed in Mackenzie's response to the testing process. For the first time in his life, the importance of standardized testing seemed to weigh on him. He no longer approached taking standardized tests as being "fun" but felt pressured to get a "good" score. He also began to experience the difference in his socio-economic status compared to his peers. Until this point, it had not bothered him that he wasn't one of the wealthy students. As he navigated the college admissions process, however, I saw an erosion in Mackenzie's self-confidence. I also observed a change in the way he viewed his peers as he became more competitive in trying to better his test scores.

3. Advanced Placement (AP) classes have changed the high school learning experience

Many independent schools and public high schools participate in the Advanced Placement Program offered by The College Board.[34] This is the same organization that manages the SAT college entrance exam. AP classes are designed to mimic college-level introductory courses. The rationale behind AP classes is they reportedly prepare students for college. Research, however, has not really examined the impact that AP classes have on students' high school experience.[35] In working with young college students, I believe that AP classes have contributed to their overall burnout with education.

That said, I agree that there are advantages to taking AP classes. One advantage is that when students score a 3, 4, or 5 on their exams, they can often earn college credit and bypass standard introductory courses when they do enroll in college. This saves on tuition costs or allows the student to explore other topics of interest. AP success (the highest scores, of course) also stands out to college admissions officers who see this an indicator that students who have done well are focused and prepared to study.

The disadvantage of AP classes is that they follow an outline so students can pass AP exams administered at the end of the semester or term. The focus is teaching to the test and not necessarily engaging students creatively or experientially in the subject matter.

So when Mackenzie announced that he was enrolling in AP classes his junior year, it brought back memories of his "coloring inside the lines" experience in first grade. When I asked him why he was interested in taking AP classes, he really did not have a formulated reason other than that he "needed" to take AP classes because a number of his peers were doing so. Some of his classmates were taking up to five AP classes at a time, which I questioned due to the academic workload. Mackenzie enrolled in no more than two each semester both junior and senior year, but the homework required for AP classes was significant.

What distressed me most about his decision to enroll in AP classes was that it was part of an overall pattern of behavior where he felt pressure to "check all the boxes" for getting into the "best" college. Taking AP classes was not about learning, but rather the need to play the college game with the rest of his peers.

More alarming, was by junior year, Mackenzie had lost his desire to learn. He was no longer curious and appeared disengaged in most of the subjects he studied. Since we were paying for private school tuition, this was disheartening and troubling for me. It was like seeing a stranger. He appeared to be going through the motions because that was what was expected of him.

In reflecting on his high school experience, I believe that what was needed for Mackenzie and many of his peers was social-emotional learning and support from the school. Teens need metacognitive skills to begin thinking of themselves as the agents of their own learning process —deepening their understanding of their own role in classroom communities, moving them from a passive to active role as academic learners, and connecting their lives to meaningful contributions outside the classroom."[36] This type of learning is sadly missing at most high schools across the nation.

Safety schools versus reach schools

Exploring college options has become increasingly important, with a focus on identifying "safety" schools—colleges that students will most likely be admitted to and "reach" schools—colleges that students have little chance of being admitted to. This has led to a mentality adopted by both students and parents of getting into the "best school." For the sake of clarity, I offer the definition of best schools as those institutions that accept 25% or less of their applicants each year. You should also know that students enrolling in the "best schools" represent only 3% of college going students in the country.

The college search process kicked off in full-swing the fall semester of Mackenzie's junior year. I watched with dismay as he got caught up in the college admissions madness.

Like many of his peers, Mackenzie was engaged in other activities outside his academic studies, including competing in varsity sports, volunteering for Big Brothers Big Sisters, and participating in student organizations. Adding college search activities to his already full schedule led to more anxiety and stress.

(A proud Mom aside here...) Mackenzie was one of a few students in the history of the school who qualified for state competition in three sports—cross country, swimming, and track in both junior and senior year. I learned late in the college search process that being a student athlete could be a plus when applying to selective colleges. This insider tip came from a parent who had invested significant resources to send her son to summer sports camps where college coaches would scout for talented athletes (and yes, it worked—her son was admitted to one of the Ivy League universities where he ran track).

Junior-year track

Once again, I was struck by the role that socio-economic status played in the college admissions process.

At the beginning of his junior year, Mackenzie was assigned a seasoned college counselor very knowledgeable of the college admissions process. They began meeting at regular intervals with the goal of developing a list of college options for him to explore.

Based on a survey that he completed, his Myers-Briggs Type Indicator (MBTI) results, and one-on-one conversations, the college counselor developed a list of colleges for Mackenzie to research.[37] The list was shared with us and we were invited to provide feedback.

Mackenzie's initial list of potential college options was quite lengthy. His interests were very broad and it was apparent that he was unclear as to what he might want to study in college—anything from sports marketing to engineering.

This lack of clarity is typical of many high school students. Our current K-12 education system does not prepare students for clarifying potential vocational interests, so when students begin to explore colleges, they don't often have a clear idea of what they might want to study as a major or degree.

Like the previous two years, Mike and I were invited to attend a parent information session for parents of juniors. The head of USN spoke at the meeting and strongly encouraged us to not worry so much about where our child would apply to college, but to enjoy time with them as they engaged in the college search process. He had gone through the process with his two children and knew the angst that families experience during the college search. Take a breath, relax, was the message.

It was also recommended that if families were traveling for vacation and visiting an area where there was a college, that we consider scheduling a campus tour and attending an information session. By engaging in this process, students would be able to compare colleges and begin to identify whether they had an interest in large or small schools, urban or residential campuses, public institutions or selective private schools, etc.

4. College visits are an investment of time and money

Following this advice, we began to include college visits as part of family travel.

During the winter break, we were in southern California visiting family for the holidays, so we traveled to Los Angeles to check out several college campuses, including the Claremont schools Pomona and Pitzer, Harvey Mudd, the University of Southern California (USC), the

University of California, Los Angeles (UCLA), and Occidental. All the colleges were closed for winter break, but we had the opportunity to walk around the campuses.

From our meandering, reading downloaded admissions campus guides, and research on the Internet, we got a general sense of the schools' relative to size and gained an overall impression of each school. It was fun to explore different campuses as a family. Mackenzie's younger brother, Stuart, benefited as well. Being three years behind Mackenzie in school, he had an early opportunity to compare schools which would help him when it came time for his own college search. I particularly enjoyed seeing the different campuses. I was familiar with many of these institutions from my work in higher education, but had never visited them.

First college visit - snowed out!

Spring break found the family traveling to multiple campuses to attend information sessions, sometimes visiting two colleges on the same day. Planning these visits required creating a matrix on our home office whiteboard with information on the days of the week, times of the day information sessions were offered, and distances between schools. The matrix helped us create a travel itinerary that maximized our time and "allowed" multiple visits per day. In total, we visited ten campuses over six days including Johns Hopkins, William & Mary, University of Virginia (UVA), University of Richmond, Duke, University of North Carolina at Chapel Hill (UNC), Elon, Wake Forest, and Davidson College. And it did not end there. During his senior year, Mackenzie visited the University of Kansas (my alma mater), Occidental, USC, Pomona, Tulane, and the University of Miami.

It was evident to me from his indecision, that Mackenzie was really struggling with the college search. He was unclear as to what he wanted to study and what college or university would be a "fit" for his interests. He was going through the motions like the rest of his peers. He was on a treadmill and could not get off. This was alarming because his behavior was mirrored in my daily work with students at Vanderbilt University. Students visiting the undergraduate career services office at Vanderbilt were typically stressed and often unclear as to the reason why they were in college. Only that it was "expected" (by their parents).

> I think that one of the biggest challenges for this generation of parents and their children is that it seems harder for parents to let their students struggle. And so, sometimes anxiety increases when you don't feel you can handle something hard that has come your way, or that you don't know the answer to, or that seems unknown.
> —Cristin Viebranz, USN College Counselor 2003-2020

So what did I do? I continued to be a part of this crazy process. As a parent, it is easy to get caught up in wanting to support your child. I wanted Mackenzie to have opportunities like the rest of his peers and did not want to disappoint him. Mike and I continued to finance his college search and paid for numerous college application fees without proactively addressing the underlying issues that he was dealing with that resulted in his indecision. In my defense, I did encourage Mackenzie to seek counseling from a personal counselor contracted by the school to help students with anxiety and stress. He chose not to and I did not press him to do so.

College rankings are part of the game

College admissions changed forever when the *US News and World Report* college rankings system was introduced in the 1980's. The higher a college ranks on this exclusive list, the more students they can recruit and, even better, the more students they can reject, which drives up their rankings. Does this make any sense?

Smart schools quickly saw the value of exclusivity and discovered if they could adjust the right data, their ranking would go up. If higher ed is a business, landing a top 25 spot is kind of like reaching a spot on the Fortune 500 which can yield more alumni donations and academic bragging rights.

One practice that contributes to increased selectivity in college admissions has been the use of the Common App. Prospective students are able to apply to over 900 colleges and universities using this on-line application. They simply indicate where they want their applications to be submitted by the click of a button and their materials are electronically sent to the schools for consideration. By making it easier to apply, applications have increased at many colleges and universities. However, the number of students admitted have largely remained the same so it appears that universities have become more selective by their lower acceptance rates.

This practice has also resulted in students applying to colleges and schools that are not only "safety schools" but also "reach schools."

Despite the ease of applying to multiple colleges, students are frequently asked to submit responses to supplemental questions that individual colleges and universities pose as part of their own application and admissions processes. The additional requirements are an overlooked burden that is only realized after the decision has been made to apply to a high number of schools.

This was the case for Mackenzie. In the end, he applied to 17 schools. Seventeen! His first application was to Claremont-McKenna in which he sought Early Decision. Mackenzie was part of a large number of seniors from his school who submitted applications in the early fall seeking "Early Action" or "Early Decision." [38]

The topic of Early Action (EA) and Early Decision (ED) could be an entire chapter in itself as I believe it is another piece in the college admissions game. What I will say on the topic is that selective colleges and universities use ED and EA to ensure enrollment.

The upside for students who choose to apply ED is that they significantly improve their chances for admission to a selective college. The downside: 1) students don't know what financial aid they will receive from the school when they are admitted through the early decision process; and 2) students agree to withdraw their applications for consideration at other colleges and universities when they are admitted ED, greatly limiting their options early in their senior year.

> Marketing by colleges has become much more sophisticated. What you see from colleges through their emails, publications, social media presence, is that they are in somewhat of an arms race with each other. Additionally, *US News and World Report* is another huge player who has become more and more important because of their college rankings and the press coverage those rankings receive. For instance, because the acceptance rate for a college is part of some of their ranking metric, colleges have been influenced to increase the number of applications they receive to lower their acceptance rates.
> — Cristin Viebranz, USN College Counselor 2003-2020

Mackenzie heard back from Claremont-McKenna in December that he was denied admission. This led to a frenzy of college applications submitted in January and February to other colleges and universities on his list. And if you recall, there were 16 others!

By the first of April, Mackenzie had been admitted to seven of the 16 schools and waitlisted at one school—Washington University in St Louis. Most of the schools he had been admitted to were his "safety schools" with the exception of Wash U, which he has considered a "reach school."

The role and purpose of the waitlist

So what does it mean to be waitlisted?[39]

The waitlist is another part of the college admissions game. The process works this way: to create a pool of qualified students that admissions can tap if the school has not met enrollment targets by May 1st, they will make waitlist offers to a number of students who were not initially admitted. Students are required to either accept or decline a waitlist offer, and it must be prior to May 1st—which is the deadline for students to accept an admissions offer and pay their enrollment deposit. Based on the yield of accepted students, colleges and universities will turn to waitlists in May and throughout the summer, and make admission offers to students in order to hit their enrollment target. A waitlist student can potentially be offered admission anytime after May 1st to the beginning of the start of a college term.

There are challenges of waitlist offers for students. They may have committed to attend another school and paid non-refundable deposits, including housing deposits. Financial aid awards are usually less from the waitlist school, as funds have already been awarded to the first round of admitted students. For some students, however, a waitlist offer is an opportunity to attend one of their dream schools. "Mom and Dad will understand losing the non-refundable deposit." And what's the big deal about financial aid?!?

As my sons often say, "Right...!"

All applications are not created equal

Out of the "rankings or bust" mentality rose a cottage industry of third-party players. Some promised to create advantages for students via academic coaching and creating business plans to help parents choose the right sports, volunteer activities, or other experiences to make their students more competitive. Others marketed their direct connections to university decision makers who might be persuaded to admit a student if the right amount of money (donations) was placed on the table.

The Varsity Blues scandal put a spotlight on these practices in college admissions and proved (most people already knew this) there are sometimes two paths for applicants—one for people with money, one for everyone else. So far, more than 50 parents (some are celebrities and business tycoons), coaches, and test administrators have been indicted for everything from cheating on entrance exams to bribing athletic coaches. A few have gone to jail.

But not all bribes are illegal. Consider that businessman Louis DeJoy gave Duke University $2.2 million while his son was enrolled there and that Jared Kushner was admitted to Harvard after his father gave the storied Ivy school $2.5 million.[40]

Where is the line and how do parents know when they've crossed it?

That gets a little murky.

There are other ways to gain advantage in the college admissions process, particularly, at highly selective colleges and universities. Admission decisions will typically favor legacy applicants with connections and wealth over non-legacy applicants with few connections and limited financial means. At some of the most selective institutions, legacy applicants make up 25% of an entering first-year class. It's no wonder why colleges and universities struggle with creating diverse and inclusive communities!

At my former institution, I was flabbergasted when a parent openly admitted to me during a fall family weekend reception that she had submitted her son's application to the school without his knowledge. He was standing beside her during this conversation as she bragged about her success in getting him into this highly selective school. What's just as disconcerting is that the student decided to enroll because he hadn't been admitted to his top college choice. Hearing this just reinforced for me the unfairness of the selective admissions process. This parent helped her son cheat (unwittingly at first), and he was accepted over many other students who had submitted their own application.

Another way of creating an advantage is to hire educational consultants to complete students' college applications and write college essays. According to the head of admissions at my former institution, it is not uncommon for a family to pay $30K or more to consultants to help with college applications. Selective universities know these practices exist but few, if any, have taken steps to review and change their processes in order to address systemic cheating. By doing so, it would be a positive step in ensuring equal access for all students.

It's important to make a distinction here—not all educational consultants are alike. Many provide valuable and affordable services to families unfamiliar with the college search process. Because many high schools are not resourced to provide college counseling or are only able to provide minimal guidance, consultants can play an important role in helping families navigate the rather complex system of college admissions.

And, not surprising, the complex barriers and admissions processes discussed here can magically melt away if an applicant is an exceptional athlete who can contribute to a winning team.

5. Choosing a college is stressful

Mackenzie began the process of making a decision once he had multiple offers to consider. He had until May 1st to make a "final" selection. The fear of making a wrong decision was evident in his approach. He appeared paralyzed with indecision. After all, the college he attended would forever define his success in life, right?

Not really. But most students (and I am sad to say many parents) hold the belief that college choice equates to future success, and it is a big contributor to their overall stress and anxiety.

To help him with the decision process, we suggested creating a decision matrix—a spreadsheet listing all his options with key factors to consider, including overall cost, financial aid awards, majors available, size of school, and location. He narrowed down his choices to three schools (with input from Mike and me, since we would be on the hook financially for his decision). For both our sons, we had committed to paying for their college if we had the resources.

To our dismay, two of the schools on his list, Tulane and the University of Miami, were ones that he had not visited. We debated the value of visiting the schools in April and concluded that if we were to invest significant resources for him to attend one of these schools, campus visits would be a nominal investment. So I drove Mackenzie to visit Tulane in New Orleans, and two weeks later, Mike flew with him to visit the University of Miami.

I was hoping that the college visits would help provide clarity for Mackenzie but they did not. Up until the last day, last hour, he was conflicted as to whether to choose Tulane or Miami. In the end, he committed to attend the University of Miami.

I think what ultimately led to his decision to go to Miami was that he had received an invitation from the track and field coach to be a walk-on to the track team. No scholarships were available but the opportunity to compete as part of a NCAA Division I track program was appealing. I did not see him as a college student athlete, necessarily, but it was nice to know that he would have that opportunity.

With his decision came a big sigh of relief. It had been an exhaustive process. We were glad to be done.

College t-shirt day

Of course, we weren't. This was just the beginning in helping our son effectively launch as an adult.

In *The Launching Years. Strategies for parenting from senior year to college life*, authors Kastner and Wyatt suggest that the two years beginning senior year in high school through the first year of college can be some of the most difficult parenting years.[41] Adolescence has been elongated and parents are having to proactively parent much longer. Since military service, marriage, and employment are no longer the norm after high school, young people ages 18-25 are considered 'emerging adults'.[42]

Hindsight is 20/20

I discovered Kastner's and Wyatt's work as part of my research for this book and it has been beneficial in providing insight into what I experienced during Mackenzie's senior year. The recommendations and strategies offered by the authors have also prepared me for what might be next. This book is a must-read for any parent of a college-bound student.

I close with two quotes from Kastner and Wyatt that I encourage you to take to heart:

"Launching a child to college can feel as if it's one of our last hands-on parenting acts. The college choice appears to be our child's link to the future, and, hoping to control as much as we can, we want it to be the best possible link. Invested in our child's future, we start to view college choice as the key to everything we want for our child, when in fact, no set of empirical data has been able to establish that where a young person attends college automatically correlates with success. What does correlate with eventual occupational success is the number of years of higher education; it matters that young people finish their degrees, but the specific college has no statistical significance, nor interestingly enough, do grades in high school or college."

"We know, of course, that [the college application process] doesn't divide seniors into the winners and the losers, but anxiety can skew our thinking. Though it's often covert or unconscious, parents at this juncture are comparing themselves by comparing their children's flight patterns toward various college choices. Seniors do it, too."

What You Can Do

1. Read the article "Reclaiming Senior Year." The author, Nancy Faust Sizer, taught in private schools for many years and offers insight into what is really happening during your student's senior year.[43]
2. Determine the role you would like to play in your young adult's college search—observer, active partner, or driving force—and consider the impact you will have based on level of involvement.
3. Discuss and arrange for counseling for your young adult if you are concerned about their well-being.

Notes

Am I Too Late?

Chapter 4
Ready or Not?

Most ambitions are either achieved or abandoned; either way, they belong to the past. The future, instead of the ladder toward the goals of life, flattens out into a perpetual present. Money, status, all the vanities the preacher of Ecclesiastes describes hold so little interest: a chasing after wind, indeed.

—from When Breath Becomes Air, Paul Kalanithi

My "mom" radar was on high alert.

Earlier in the week, Mike and I had received an email invitation from one of Mackenzie's AP teachers at USN to meet with him at school as he had a "matter he would like to discuss with the two of us."

We were now sitting facing him in his office wondering what this was about.

"I don't get it, " he said. "Maybe you can help me."

Mike and I exchanged worried glances.

He continued, "I see incredible potential in Mackenzie, but for some reason, he seems disconnected to learning in the class. He is doing the minimum just to get a decent grade but I know that he has the capacity to do better. Are you able to provide some insight into how I can engage him more deeply in the classroom conversation? What has proven helpful in his other classes?"

At this point in Mackenzie's senior year, I didn't have an answer. There had been only a couple of classes that he had really connected to earlier on in high school—one was his AP Environmental Science class. His lack of engagement with his education had increasingly been a point of concern for me. Hearing his AP teacher echo what I had been thinking for the past three years was disheartening and alarming at the same time. I suspected that Mackenzie was suffering from burnout.

He had lost interest in school but, because of his competitive nature, did just enough to keep up with his fellow classmates and their focus on grades. I wasn't sure what could be done to help him regain his love for learning. It clearly was not going to be this AP class or this dedicated teacher.

Would college be the answer?

I didn't think so.

Reasons students go to college

Everyday, in my work at Vanderbilt, I saw students' struggling to answer the question of why they were in college. Surveys of entering freshmen conducted by the Vanderbilt Institutional Research Group found that students reported that their number one reason for college was to secure a good job. However, Michael Horn and Bob Moesta, co-authors of *Choosing College: How to Make Better Learning Decisions Throughout Your Life,* suggest that it is important to look at the motivation behind the student's college choice to better understand their decision.

They argue that "... a simple survey misses the complexity of what is driving people's choices. When confronted with a set of possible responses, people often fill in what they think they are supposed to say—or, in this case, what their parents might say—even if it doesn't fully align with their reasons. Often, a set of responses doesn't contain what's driving someone to make a decision—or it misses the multifaceted reasons why people choose something."[44]

Their research found that students choose college for five major reasons:

To get into their best college;
To do what's expected of them;
To get away;
To step it up; and
To extend themselves.

They write, "For example, students looking to get into their best college or university often want to gain access to a network and entry-level opportunities that will lead to a good-paying job in the future. But their driving motivation is much more about getting into college, less about what college will help them do or attain. These students are swayed by everything from the opportunity to have the "classic college" experience on a beautiful brick-and-mortar campus to the opportunity to reinvent themselves among new people at a prestigious place that is highly regarded."

From my work in career services at several different colleges and universities, both public and private, I have found that most students don't have a clear idea of what they want to do with their life so going to college is the default option they choose. Their identity of being a "student" is all they have known since they were three years old at "pre-school," so continuing to be a "student" is familiar and an easy option to choose.

I contrast these students' reasons for attending college with the "adult learners" I have worked with at both elite private schools and public state institutions. These adult undergraduates come from diverse backgrounds. Many are first in their family to attend college and are making significant sacrifices, both personal and financial, to get their degree. Their primary reason for going to college is the belief that a college degree will help them improve their chances in life.

I tend to agree with Ted Dintersmith, a former venture capitalist turned K-12 education reformer, that the primary reason why so many young adults are going to college is that is what our K-12 education system has prepared them to do. Though, I wonder, at what cost?

"With college at the top of our pecking order," Dintersmith writes in *What School Could Be*, "our K-12 schools fall in line, striving to produce 'college-ready' graduates. Affluent schools grease every skid, with students locked into an AP, SAT test prep, and extracurricular arms race. Low-and middle-income schools want the same opportunities for their kids and push their students along the same college-ready path. All schools—in overt and subtle ways—condition students to equate their worth with college outcomes, with parents piling on. College isn't just a goal for most students. It's the goal for all students."[45]

"Doing school"

Unfortunately, the focus on college prep has drastically impacted students' high school experience. To meet college admissions requirements and expectations, high schools have increasingly adopted a "standardized learning" approach. Not only do we see an increasing number of students suffering from high levels of anxiety and stress, we also see an educational system that "crushes" innovation and creativity out of them. And like Mackenzie, they are often disengaged in learning, going through the motions of "doing" school.

To address this crisis, Dintersmith suggests a reimagination of education; one where learning is self-directed and where student engagement and innovation occur in classrooms and educational settings that help students develop "purpose, agency, essential skills sets and mindsets, and deep knowledge." When these are part of the educational model, Dintersmith found from his research, young people have the ability to work on complex problems and make a difference in the communities they are part of.

Mackenzie would have benefited from this approach during high school. Early on, through his Montessori education, he thrived when his learning was self-directed. When he transitioned to USN, he entered a learning environment that was "other-directed." He also became a casualty of an educational system that reinforced the message that the only viable option after high school graduation is to go to college.

In today's highly regarded public and private high schools, there is little work being done to help students think about alternative learning opportunities, and there is little to no emphasis on considering the option of taking time off for a year or two to work or volunteer— alternatives that would offer students the chance to gain experience and perspective in choosing a college and a major to study.

As a result, students are pressured to pursue college because other options are less desirable. Most do not want to join the military and they are shamed if they consider community college or technical or vocational training (even if it is free).

What's left? Four years of college!

An important question to ask

One of the biggest mistakes that I made during Mackenzie's high school years, particularly his senior year, was to not sit down with him and simply ask the question: "Do you want to go to college?" Followed by "Why do you want to go to college?" and "What do you want to learn while you are there?"

From the indecision reflected in Mackenzie's college search process, I recognized he was not ready for college.

I offer the advice provided by Kastner in *The Launching Years*, "A key task for parents is to assess whether your senior is ready, mature, and motivated to take advantage of college resources next year. Ask yourself, 'What will my child benefit most from for the next period of time?' Keep in mind that it is a fallacy to base success ... on the caliber of a child's college-admission ticket and that an individual's future is built more on values, drive, and the quality of engagement in school and life than a 4.0 GPA. Make the step to college an informed step, not a lock-step, and create a plan where something wonderful will happen for your child."

More importantly, this is a time when we can begin to address the stress that our young adults are experiencing. The increasing number of students who are struggling with mental health and emotional well-being issues is alarming. The level of chronic stress beginning in middle school through high school is taking its toll on our young adults and they are becoming fragile at a time when resiliency is needed to adapt to the rapidly changing world and workplace.

If we are to support a society where we want innovation, it is imperative that we begin early on to stress the importance of having time to just "think." There is an inability to focus for long periods by our youth, college students, and new professionals. They remain distracted by constant digital messaging and receive instant gratification by a post. This results in a short attention span and lack of patience. The current trend to integrate mindfulness activities in schools across the US is a positive step in connecting individuals with themselves, freeing the mind of distractions, and the constant push to be "busy" and "do" and "plan."

A tsunami of stress and anxiety

Despite efforts like mindfulness training in schools, the anxiety and stress that high school students experience does not miraculously just disappear when they attend college. Rather it has created a fragility in incoming college students that has led to colleges' current struggle with ways to address the health and well-being of first-year students. College presidents are looking to K-12 leaders to address this issue.

As part of my research for this book, I interviewed Tim Bazemore, Head of Catlin Gabel School, an independent K-12 school in Portland, Oregon. Tim is part of an effort, the Mastery Transcript Consortium (MTC), to change high school transcripts from the current focus on grades to a focus on evaluating students' learning or competencies in mastering different concepts being taught.[46]

Changing the way high schools evaluate students requires buy-in from higher education leaders. Tim conducted interviews with a number of college presidents to get their feedback. He shared with me that, during these meetings, almost every single college president asked him about "what private schools like Catlin Gabel were doing to address the well-being of students." They said this was the number one issue that was creating significant challenges on their respective campuses.

I doubt that there will be overnight reform to address these issues in secondary schools. The good news is that universities are working hard to provide necessary support for students. For example, while I was at Vanderbilt, a CARE team of faculty and staff was established to handle students in crises. In recent years, the university has opened a Center for Student Wellbeing, joining a number of other colleges and universities seeking to address students' emotional and mental health. PSU, where I currently work, is consistently focused on ensuring that students' mental health and emotional well-being are supported throughout their college studies.

Making sense of college

One solution to decrease stress and anxiety in students would be for high schools to help them define meaning and building purpose in their lives as part of the college search process.

Why is this important?

As human beings, we seek meaning in our lives. We seek to make sense out of things; "… we seek pattern, order, coherence, and relation in the disparate elements of our experience. If life is perceived as only fragmented and chaotic, we suffer confusion, distress, stagnation, and despair."[47] This is what high school students are experiencing.

Sharon Daloz Parks, in her book *Big Questions. Worthy Dreams. Mentoring Young Adults in Their Search for Meaning, Purpose, and Faith*, suggests that the big questions whose answers define adulthood include **purpose, vocation, and belonging**. She suggests that young adults be asked questions that "… offer bridges to a worthy dream of a life distinctively one's own."

Providing students an opportunity to reflect on questions that they inherently ask in their adult quest would have a significant impact on their approach to the college search and decision process. By encouraging students to reflect on their lives in a holistic way, we would help them develop a college plan that is aligned with their purpose. This approach could be easily integrated into the college planning process, if deemed a priority.

Parks offers questions that would be helpful for students to reflect upon. Here are a few:

- Who do I really want to become?
- How do I work toward something when I don't even know what it is?
- What are the values and limitations of my culture?
- Who am I as a sexual being?
- Do my actions make any real difference in the bigger scheme of things?
- What is my society, or life, or God, asking of me? Anything?
- What is the meaning of money? How much is enough?
- Am I wasting time I'll regret later?
- What constitutes meaningful work?
- What do I want the future to look like—for me, for others, for my planet?
- What is my religion? Do I need one?
- What are my real talents, preferences, skills, and longings?
- When do I feel most alive?

- Where can I be creative?
- What are my fears?
- How am I complicit in patterns of injustice?
- Will I always be stereotyped?
- What do I really want to learn?
- Where do I want to put my stake in the ground and invest my life?

Throughout our lives, we continue to seek answers to questions of purpose and meaning—most often raised during times of change and transition. The high school to college transition is a critical time for young adults.

From my experience in higher education, allowing students to define their purpose has not been integrated into their college experience. It's a nice marketing tag-line along with other grandiose mission statements like: "prepare students to think broadly, deeply and critically, and to contribute to the world" (Stanford); "challenge students to develop those habits of intellect and imagination that will prepare them for learning and leadership throughout their lives" (Colorado College); "to educate the citizens and citizen-leaders for our society" (Harvard); and "prepare students for lives of service, civic engagement, and ethical leadership" (Princeton).

Becoming part of the herd

So what happens when students arrive to college stressed, lacking direction, and a sense of purpose?

They often adopt a "herd" mentality and work to escape their stress (and pain) using alcohol and drugs.

To better understand what I mean by "herd mentality," I recommend William Deresiewicz's book, *Excellent Sheep: The Miseducation of the American Elite and the Way to a Meaningful Life*.[48] He details what happens to many young adults who attend elite institutions in the US and the "herd mentality" that results. They lack purpose and direction, so their default is to become part of the "herd" not willing to take risks. They follow their peers in pursuing internships and full-time jobs in industries like consulting and finance, and often major in subjects that they are not interested in because they think it will help them get a better job.

I saw evidence of this firsthand in my work at Vanderbilt University and I did not want this for my son. I was reluctant to invest in his college education when he did not have a clear reason for being there.

Compounding students' emotional and mental health is the partying culture that has become pervasive on many US college campuses. To find a release from the stress and pressures they feel, many young adults engage in risky behaviors. Binge drinking, hookup culture, and reports of sexual assaults are on the rise. It is not uncommon for students to begin partying on Thursday night and not stop until Sunday evening. You may be thinking, "No big deal. Partying on college campuses has been happening for years. This is not a new phenomenon."

Declining student resilience has become a significant problem for college personnel

To understand the difference, I encourage you to read *Binge. What Your College Student Won't Tell You.*[49] Author Barrett Seaman provides a sobering analysis of the partying culture and its impact on college campuses. My mentor and former supervisor, Associate Provost Howard Sandler, shared this resource as part of my professional development at Vanderbilt University. It provided significant insight into what was happening not only at Vanderbilt but at other campuses across the US.

One example of partying culture that particularly sticks out in my memory was beach weekend on campus. One spring, I was walking to a meeting when I noticed a number of beautifully decorated ice coolers outside one of the sororities on campus. Standing beside the coolers were young women excitedly talking to each other, laughing, and clearly having a good time.

When I asked a colleague who was familiar with campus Greek Life about what I had just seen, she shared with me that this was the annual beach weekend for fraternities and sororities. The yearly ritual involved sorority "girls" inviting fraternity "boys" (whom they did not necessarily know) for a weekend on the beach. It was expected that the girls would provide all the alcohol for the weekend as well as sex. I was flabbergasted! "Why would bright, intelligent young women choose to engage in this risky and unhealthy behavior," I wondered. When I expressed my dismay to my colleague, she responded that this was part of the campus culture. That struck me as sad.

Universities known for their party cultures typically have a significant number of students that belong to fraternities or sororities. When I began my tenure at Vanderbilt, approximately 45% of the students pledged to a Greek organization. To the university's credit, as it sought to admit students from different socio-economic backgrounds in efforts to diversify its student body, Greek membership declined. In 2018-2019, approximately 35% of all students belonged to a Greek organization. Unfortunately, with one-third of the student population being Greek, partying continues to be pervasive throughout students' experience. And this continues to impact students' overall well-being.

Jumping off the treadmill

My biggest fear was that Mackenzie was headed down a similar path that I was seeing in students at Vanderbilt. He was stressed, desperately running on a treadmill that we have inadvertently created for college-bound students, and unable to jump off or stop. I did not want him to become as fragile as the students we were seeing in our office daily. I could easily see him follow a pattern where he would engage in risky behaviors and that concerned me. The University of Miami had a strong Greek culture and was also known for its partying. A fact that I was sure was not lost on my son.

I did not want Mackenzie to become part of the "herd," drifting, uninspired with no purpose or path and I didn't want to fund his education while he was deciding what he wanted to do.

Fortunately, Mackenzie recognized the need for time away from school. But would the University of Miami value this decision?

What You Can Do

1. Sit down with your young adult and ask:
   - Do you want to go to college?
   - Why do you want to go?
   - What do you want to learn?
2. Ask your young adult if they have been afraid to pursue something in their life because it did not fit with the expectations of themselves and others. What was it?
3. Consider the readiness of your young adult to attend college and remind yourself that there are many paths they can take to be happy and successful.

Notes

Am I Too Late?

Part II

The Journey

Am I Too Late?

Chapter 5
Time to Explore the Gap Year

LEAVING HOME
This is the setting out.
The leaving of everything behind.
Leaving the social milieu. The preconceptions.
The definitions. The language.
The narrowed field of vision. The expectations.
No longer expecting relationships, memories, words,
or letters to mean what they used to mean.
To be, in a word: Open.

—Rabbi Lawrence Kushner

Sometimes as parents, we are challenged in moments when we should share our infinite wisdom (usually unsolicited) with our children or when we should just listen to their thoughts without judgement. It's a tricky dance and we don't always get it right. It's easier to tell than to listen.

One evening in January of Mackenzie's senior year was one of those moments.

Mackenzie had just gotten home from swim practice and was preparing to have dinner, followed by college applications and homework. I was sitting at the kitchen table responding to work emails on my laptop.

"Mom, I am thinking about taking a gap year," he said.

His words had caught me off guard and I looked up. I wasn't exactly sure how to respond to this news.

Seeking to understand why he was considering this option, I asked, "Why do you want to take a gap year?"

To this day, I remember his answer. "I would like to read for fun again, Mom. Not just read stuff required for class. I would like to have time to read things that I am interested in learning about without sitting in a classroom." The expression on his face was one of sadness and fatigue.

I'm so glad I listened. It was at this moment, I felt a spark of hope. I had been worried about Mackenzie and felt that he had lost himself in the process of "doing school."[50] A gap year might be what he needed to regain a sense of wholeness.

Mike's immediate reaction to the idea, however, was the opposite of mine. In hearing what Mackenzie was thinking, Mike replied, "You can't do that! You might not go back! I don't think that is a good idea!"

In talking with other parents of college-bound students, this is the frequent knee-jerk reaction when the topic of taking time off is raised, and it is based on fear. But what are we truly afraid of? That our child will lose ground compared to their peers? That our child will lose their impetus to study? That our child will have difficulty settling back into the routine of school? That our child will not be successful? That our child ... (substitute your worst fears here).

We also wonder "what will it cost?"

To address Mike's concerns, I knew he needed information. This is when I first began to research the topic of gap years. A handful of students that I had worked with at Colorado College had taken gap years, so I had heard the term, but had limited understanding of what the experience entailed. I also knew from hosting international students while I was at CC that it was common for young adults in Europe to take time off before starting college or work. My perception about a gap year was this: wealthy young adults backpacking around Europe for a year or volunteering in a third world country.

But was this really true?

To better understand the gap year and its impact, I read multiple books and articles on the subject. I conducted interviews with other "gappers" (as they are often called), high school college counselors, and a number of my son's peers who had gone directly to college. I even had the opportunity to interview a former college president who had worked at both private and public universities.

From my research, firsthand observations about my son's experience, and more than twenty years' experience working with traditional college-age students, I have formed a strong opinion about the value of taking time out to engage in alternative learning before enrolling in a college or university.

A gap year should be the default next step after high school graduation for many college-bound students.

A gap year focuses on alternative learning

The term "gap year" is one that has mixed support, but for now it is the one most used when describing the activity when a student takes time off between high school and college.

An official definition provided by the Gap Year Association (GYA) is that a gap year entails "... a semester or year of experiential learning, typically taken after high school and prior to career or post-secondary education, in order to deepen one's practical, professional, and personal awareness."[51]

The GYA is an excellent resource on gap years. Formerly known as the American Gap Association, it was founded by Ethan Knight (a fellow Oregonian and Willamette University graduate). He is a leading voice and thought leader on the gap year and its benefits. Ethan also founded Carpe Diem Education, a gap year provider based in Portland, Oregon.

Another excellent gap year resource is USA Gap Year Fairs.[52] This organization hosts fairs across the US and "... brings together reputable gap year organizations, interested students and parents, high school college counselors, and gap year experts." If you are a college-bound student or parent of a college-bound student, I highly recommend checking to see if there is a fair being hosted near you and attending to learn more about gap years.

To allay Mike's fears about Mackenzie's gap year, I recommended he read Karl Haigler and Rae Nelson's book, *The Gap Year Advantage. Helping*

*Your Child Benefit from Time Off Before or During College.*53 You will find it an excellent resource if your child is considering taking a gap year.

Gap year defined

In, *The Complete Guide to the Gap Year,* author Kristen White compares two approaches to gap years.54 In Europe, the gap year can be a year when the individual travels to a party spot where the focus is on fun. "The American system frowns on this behavior and trips of this kind are not considered meaningful gap year plans. Colleges do not grant deferrals for a year-long party; they hope that students will enjoy a break from structured academics **but will continue the learning process** through self-reflection, learning about other cultures, and finding purpose in their own lives."

Though many colleges and universities support students taking a gap year, the deferral process and expectations universities communicate regarding students' time off have an impact on how students and parents approach the gap year planning process. Acceptable plans involve activities where students are engaged in "doing something productive" for enrollment deferral to be justified. Students are "expected" to engage in worthwhile activities to forgo starting college right away.

In learning the details about the deferral process, I was struck, yet again, on the uber focus on "action." I didn't disagree with the notion of creating a plan for his year. As a career and life coach, I understood the value of Mackenzie developing a year plan with a focus on flexibility. However, it occurred to me that for him to find renewal, Mackenzie needed to be less "goal-driven" and "productive." He would benefit from the opportunity to relax, play, "live" in the moment, and take time to think.

Gap year proponents suggest that an impactful year include a volunteer or service component whether it be national or internationally-based, a structured learning experience, and work.

Susan Griffiths offers valuable advice in her book *Your Gap Year. The most comprehensive guide to an exciting and fulfilling year.*55 "Try not to get too worried by all the emphasis on taking a 'constructive' and 'structured' gap year, if all you want to do is spread your wings, travel and see what turns up. Teachers, parents, and organisations sometime go overboard in insisting that everything has to count for the future, and may fall prey to a near-obsession with what looks good on a CV. This is an aspect of culture in the highly developed west that might be usefully challenged on a backpacking trip in Cambodia and Laos or volunteer school-building scheme in Madagascar. The much maligned phrase 'university of life' contains an important truth; that life experiences and getting to know yourself better may be hard to measure on any league table but are just as educationally valuable as writing waffling essays about the semiotics of film."

How colleges view the gap year

Increasingly, colleges and universities, including some of the most selective institutions, have publicly stated that they encourage students to take a gap year. For example, Harvard University sends a letter to its entering first year class and recommends that they consider taking a gap year before starting college. Other institutions offer gap year programs or financial support for students pursuing gap years. These include: Tufts, Princeton, Florida State, University of North Carolina at Chapel Hill, and Elon.

So why are colleges and universities recommending students consider a gap year?

Because they have seen the value and benefits that have resulted from students taking a year off before starting college. To understand the impact, the GYA conducted a national alumni survey in conjunction with Temple University in 2015. Findings of the survey were published on the GYA web site along with data on gap years from other researchers.[56] I have taken the liberty of sorting these benefits into four categories.

Employment
- **Working in groups**. In today's work environment, people who work best with others—often denoted as having Emotional Intelligence (EQ rather than IQ)—tend to be more successful. In all regards, a gap year will challenge the student to work better with a more diverse array of people.

- **Re-igniting a sense of curiosity for learning** through real-life situations and exploring possible careers through hands on field-work. Takes a student out of "park" and helps put them into "drive."
- **Creative problem-solving** by taking any challenging situation and turning it into an opportunity—much like a broken-down bus in transit, a cultural misstep, or simply being sick while on a gap year.
- **Developing cross-cultural understanding and competence** through cultural immersion and field experiences, setting gap year graduates ahead of other applicants.
- **Learning how to communicate** when there are different basic vocabularies as a vital tool gained on a gap year.

Academic completion
- For gap year year alumni, the gap year often
  - ❖ solves issues of academic burnout with healthy choices and satisfy multiple learning types.
  - ❖ allows students to go to college with a purpose, not arbitrarily because it is what society recommends.
  - ❖ provides alumni with practical field experience that is applied and referenced to university learning.
  - ❖ allows alumni to use their immersion experience to fuel better admissions essays, and even change their major focus of study after gaining clarity and purpose.
- Gap year alumni are more likely to be supported with scholarships to engage in further civic engagement, national and international university studies.

World view
- Understand how different environments inform cultural foundations and shape relationships among the earth and local communities.
- Internationalize perspective on 'living'—how it is done and what is viewed as successful in other cultures.
- Laugh at the many cultural-difference-snafus (e.g., finding out you just told your host family in Spanish that you are "pregnant" instead of "embarrassed").
- Understand what it means to be a global citizen and own the responsibility that this means in an increasingly multicultural landscape.

Career development

- Identify and eliminate interests to best direct a major study that results in a deeply invested college-to-career future.
- Take the opportunity to apply the past 12 years of academic classroom knowledge to relevant experiences and studies—thus gaining clarity about career ambitions both favorable and unfavorable.
- Evaluate personal values and identify one's own 'best' way of living.
- Create one's own version of "success" rather than that offered by running the routine.
- Explore comfort zones and the self by doing something challenging. Pushing comfort zones allows one to better understand the self and truly know what they are capable of.
- Increasing ownership for one's own life-direction.
- A well-structured gap year program can be part of the lifelong education process and induce a profound contribution to an individual's personal development.

If you are concerned that your child might not go back to college, the survey found that 90% of students enrolled in college immediately following their gap year. Only 12% ended up changing their mind about the school they originally planned to attend. Compare these findings to the fact that 30% of first-year students transferred or dropped out of college.

Research data also revealed that gap year students outperformed their peers academically. They typically graduated within four years, which is not the norm for most college graduates today, and overwhelmingly reported satisfaction with their jobs. Another resource I found helpful in understanding the value of the gap year was Joseph O'Shea's book, *Gap Year. How Delaying College Changes People in Ways the World Needs*. His research looked at how gap years pedagogically helped people learn, what role they played in personal development, and how gap years fit into the discussion of "meaning making" out of life and becoming a full member of civic society.[57]

For those of you who are data-oriented, it is important to note that a majority of the data available on gap year outcomes is based on student self-reports. In an effort to better understand outcomes of the gap year from the college and university perspective, the Gap Year Research Consortium at Colorado College was launched in 2018.[58] The goal of the consortium is to "... bring together admissions deans and researchers from top colleges and universities to study the outcomes of taking an intentional gap year before college." Consortium members include Colorado College (where approximately 10% of students complete a gap year), Colby College, Duke, Florida State, Harvard, MIT, Portland State, Stanford, Tufts, and Yale.

Who is responsible for helping students build skills and competencies on campus?

Gap year students report developing skills that are considered essential core competencies by employers: problem-solving, teamwork, collaboration, professionalism, work ethic, communications, leadership, and global and multicultural fluency.[59] Though they may not realize the importance, students are developing career readiness competencies as part of the experiential learning that a gap year affords.

Compare this to higher education's approach to building essential competencies. What we see now is a segmentation on college campuses where this occurs. Instead of designing students' curricular and co-curricular experiences with a lens on developing the core competencies that help students launch after college (aka career readiness competencies), universities and colleges have created one-off experiences or programs where students may gain these skills. They often expect understaffed and underfunded career services offices at their institutions to be solely responsible for preparing students to launch after graduation.

I did mention that these offices are typically understaffed, right?

I have often wondered what student employment and graduate school outcomes might look like if universities invested in employing the same number of career services employees as they do admissions officers. Or the same number of athletic coaches and staff hired to support one NCAA Division I sport. Why not invest the same resources in helping students exit the campus and transition to life after college?

One fall, when I was considering the work that my team would be engaged in at the Vanderbilt Career Center and wondering how we could meet the expectations of all our stakeholders, I picked up the weekly campus newspaper, _The Hustler_. It ran a feature on the football program. At the time, besides the head coach, the university employed 30 additional staff to support the football team. This number did not include academic advising staff dedicated to university athletes, marketing staff dedicated to promoting the program, and let's not forget the university athletic director and associate athletic director. And how many students were on the football team? 110. Compare this to the student to staff ratio of my office at the time which was 6,800 students to 18 full-time staff. And this number did not include alumni we were asked to serve.

Unfortunately, what you find at Vanderbilt regarding staffing at career services offices is not too different than what you find at many colleges and universities. As a private institution, we were better staffed than public institutions, but still nothing to brag about when you consider the number of students we were expected to serve. What I found most challenging were the expectations of our stakeholders—parents, employers, university leaders and faculty—that students would be career (and life) ready when they graduated. And that the Career Center would be solely responsible for their successful launch.

Meeting the needs of individual students, a majority who enter college without having any idea about what they want to do when they graduate, or lack a sense of purpose, is difficult, labor-intensive, and requires significant resources.

Dreams of a more engaged curriculum to prepare students for life

One cost-effective solution for preparing students for life after college is to consider using the entire campus as a learning lab. For example, the residential campus experience, like what is offered at Vanderbilt, offers a number of experiential learning opportunities for students to acquire skills needed to be successful as they transition after college. However, rather than look at the "experience" and "teaching moments" in real-time, universities typically run "programs" for students which often have little impact. Learning is passive and not active. Students fail to connect what they are learning from their living and learning communities to skill development. These one-off types of programs are rarely aligned with the university's academic mission and are not integrated as part of the student's overall experience.

A more economical solution to preparing students for their launch post college is one where the entire institution is engaged in this effort. This would involve designing a curricular and co-curricular college experience that integrates touch-points where students gain essential skills and they are able to communicate them as part of their story.

Take leadership skill development. For a select few students, developing effective leadership skills might occur when they assume on-campus positions like being a Resident Assistant in a residence hall or being a leader of a student organization. But getting students to contextualize their leadership role rarely happens. It would greatly benefit students to think about these roles as an experiential learning opportunity filled with professional development teaching moments that reinforce critical skills acquisition. I recognize that many college students have held leadership roles while in high school but the contextualization of the experience connecting it to skills acquisition does not occur there either.

You may be wondering, what do I mean by contextualizing?

Here is an example. Students who act as admissions' tour guides have the perfect opportunity to learn how to tell their story effectively (communication skills.) This is excellent training for internship and job interviews. Unfortunately, students rarely connect the dots that this experience is part of professional development and skills acquisition. It would take little effort and relatively no cost to integrate a teaching moment or two that helps students reflect on competencies they have gained through this leadership experience. We all know the power of experiential learning, which is why integrating professional development touchpoints and teaching moments into students' college experience makes sense.

Currently, students have the opportunity to learn how to tell their story by tapping into the resources that their university career services office typically provides. These include interviewing workshops, mock interviews, and career coaching. But I would argue that this is out of context. It is difficult for students to understand and, more importantly, talk about their college experiences in a holistic manner.

This is what I found when I was working with students at Vanderbilt. They struggled to tell their stories and their narratives were often disjointed. A classic example of this was reflected in the responses to the common career coaching question and one posed in most interviews: "Tell me about yourself." Students often responded by describing the different activities that they were engaged in: "I am studying economics. I am a member of a fraternity. I am active in student organizations [insert a number of different ones here]. I am a Resident Assistant. I am currently interning at a local investment firm." Answers were usually surface level without any depth, and it was difficult to gain a sense of the student. It took a great deal of effort and time for me to get students to a point where they were able to describe their activities in terms of core competencies, such as leadership, negotiating, finance, planning, etc.

Other challenges I found that impacted students' narratives included declining resiliency, lack of clarity in purpose and identity, and overall professional communication skills.

The Five Pillars

To address these challenges at Vanderbilt, I co-led an effort with the Dean of the Ingram Commons, Dr. Francis Wcislo, to develop students' core competencies as part of the first-year student experience. All first year students lived on campus in one of ten residential houses headed up by a faculty member. Collectively, we worked to integrate key teaching moments and build activities into the living learning community with the goal of facilitating professional development and skills acquisition.

These included:

- Identity—understanding and telling your story
- Transitions—understanding change and taking action
- Opportunities—discovering paths to opportunities
- Connections—understanding relationships and networks
- Professionalism—preparing for professional interactions

The success of this effort initially looked promising. Unfortunately, senior leadership changed at the university resulting in a shift in direction, and the collaboration to create an integrated approach to building core competencies was disbanded.

It was during this time, when I was involved in the effort to change the university's approach to preparing students for life after college, that I realized more than ever that Mackenzie "needed" to take time off. The University of Miami was similar to Vanderbilt in its approach to preparing students for work and life after college. I doubted that he would gain the core competencies needed to effectively launch. Based on what I had observed while working with college students at Vanderbilt, there was a strong likelihood that he would either end up joining the herd

> One of the challenges in applying to college is that the timing is the same for everyone, but developmentally, everybody's not in the same place. I think that it's great for students to have the opportunity to step away from the structure of the academic world if they're feeling burnt out, or if it's not meaningful to them, or if they're not sure what they want to do, or what they want to major in, or if learning in a structured setting is not interesting to them.
> —Cristin Viebranz, USN College Counselor 2003-2020

of students who thought success meant going to work for a finance or consulting firm, or he would spend four years drifting through college and not be prepared to launch when he finished.

A gap year might be just the answer.

Gap years have been around for awhile

For myself, I struggle with the term "gap year." It sounds as if there is a "gap" in someone's life rather than it being just part of an individual's living and learning journey. From my research, I have found other terms for the gap experience including:

- Sabbatical year—a year off of work or school
- Vision Quest—originally used to describe rite of passage in a number of Native American cultures but has expanded to a broader definition.
- Bridge Year or foundation year—often used by educators. In fact, a handful of universities offer bridge year programs, including Princeton, Tufts, and UNC-Chapel Hill.

In Sweden, according to my friend Kerstin Ivarsson, a gap year is called "Sabbath year." Many Swedes like Kerstin take one year off between high school and college studies. That's how we met; she spent her gap year studying in the US at the University of Kansas, my alma mater.

Other terms that are an improvement over "gap year" include "launch year," "leap year," and "discovery year."

Are there risks to taking a year off?

There are more than enough naysayers who caution that students could face financial ruin or drift aimlessly thru life if they take a gap year before or during college.

Two researchers wrote an article in *Liberty Street Economics*, a publication of the Federal Reserve Bank of New York, claiming that students who take a gap year during the pandemic will lose more than $90,000 in lifetime earnings. "First, you give up a year's worth of wages that could have been earned with a college degree had you graduated a year earlier. Second, if you enter the job market a year later, it damages your entire lifetime earnings profile because you miss out on the experience and the extra push that gives your wages over your working life, creating an earnings wedge each year. In essence, entering the job market a year later puts you behind for your entire career and you never really catch up."[60]

Not so fast.

A few months later, a Forbes article claimed that the Fed piece was full of faulty assumptions including the idea that all students graduate in four years. "Over 40 percent of first-time, full-time students who started college in the fall of 2012 failed to graduate from four-year programs within six years, according to the National Student Clearinghouse Research Center. Students who are in the top income quartile are more likely to graduate—the rate is 62 percent, but the graduation rate for individuals in the bottom income quartile is a catastrophic 13 percent."[61]

To the contrary, the author says taking a gap year can actually improve the student graduation rate.

"If students take a gap year where they have a clear plan in place that is time-bound—meaning at the end of the year or two they will apply to receive more formal education—they can build passion and purpose and create a deeper intrinsic sense for why they should go to college and how it will help them. By enrolling with that sense of purpose, our research showed that they have a much greater likelihood of graduating."[62]

What if my learner is not a risk taker?

Taking time off or delaying college is not the norm and may still be considered unconventional and risky to some. But life is full of risks and chaos. The lives of some students are planned from the time they were infants all the way through college, but doesn't mean they will be successful or happy.

There may be risks to not taking risks

Sam McRoberts, in an article for Entrepreneur, claims that "Taking risks may seem scary, but risk is the moat standing between you and true success." [63]

He posits that most people are uncomfortable with taking risks, but that anyone can be a risk taker through practice and by taking small risks. He says "the elimination of risks is a guarantee of failure" and that the key to risk-taking is taking calculated risks. "Knowing the odds, as specifically as possible, is the key to choosing the *right* risks to take."

According to McRoberts, risk takers are also happier and have fewer regrets in life. This claim is echoed in the work of Australian palliative care nurse Bronnie Ware, who wrote *Top Five Wishes of the Dying,* where she discusses the top regrets in life of her patients: [64]

- I wish I'd had the courage to live a life true to myself, not the life others expected of me
- I wish I hadn't worked so much
- I wish I'd had the courage to express my feelings
- I wish I had stayed in touch with my friends
- I wish that I had let myself be happier

In his book *Greenlights*, author and actor Matthew McConaughey discusses life as a series of traffic lights that tell us when to go, stop, or wait. He tells the story about not knowing what to do after he graduated from high school so mom had him apply for an exchange program in Australia sponsored by the local Rotary Club. He had visions of living on the beach in Sydney and chasing girls for a year, but when he arrived, he discovered the host family was a controlling dysfunctional mess that lived in the boonies, hours from the closest city or beach. Their relationship became so turbulent that it almost came to blows, and they quit speaking the last weeks before he moved to another host family.

McConaughey says the whole experience was a "green light" for him.

"Yeah, I was forced into a winter. Forced to look inside myself because I didn't have anyone else. I didn't have anything else. I'd lost my crutches. No mom and dad, no friends, no girlfriend, no straight A's, no phone, no truck, no "Most Handsome." He said "It was a year that shaped who I am today. A year when I found myself because I was forced to." [65]

Let's call it a "learning journey"

Interestingly enough, as COVID-19 was spreading across the US and the world with no end in sight, many young adults were engaged in the process of making their college decision about where they planned to attend. Taking a gap year became the leading headline during this time as an alternative to attending college, since it was clear that higher education would be disrupted for the next academic year or longer.

Now that there is so much interest in "gap years," it is a good time to re-name the experience. I propose that "learning journey" be adopted. It is a term that Margaret Wheatley and Deborah Frieze use in their book *Walk Out, Walk On. A Learning Journey into Communities Daring to Live the Future Now.*[66]

"Walk Outs Who Walk On" is a phrase first used in India to describe a network of young people who had chosen to leave school. "They didn't consider themselves 'dropouts,' a negative label assigned to them by the school system. They left school (Walk Out) because they wanted to be learners, not passive students. They walked on to discover many ways they could contribute to creating change in their world."

Wheatley and Frieze maintain that it takes courage for an individual to leave home (walk out) in order to walk on—that by doing so, an individual is able to engage in a learning journey which often leads them to contribute to their communities or society in meaningful ways.

"We have to be brave enough to explore our questions, to cultivate dissatisfaction with the present state of things, to notice what disturbs us, what feels unfair, terrible, heartbreaking," Wheatley and Frieze advocate.

"We have to be unafraid to look reality in the eye and notice what's really going on. If what we see opens our hearts, this is a good thing, because that's where our courage is found. With open hearts, we can bravely begin searching. We can go into the world with our questions, carried by our yearning to find a simpler and more effective way to live life and to benefit more people."

Whatever the term we use to describe the gap year experience, the learning that occurs when one "immerses" themselves in the activity of living and learning outside a classroom is excellent preparation for life and can help effectively launch a young person into adulthood.

What You Can Do

1. Ask your young adult the question: "Are there interests and passions from your childhood that you've lost that you would like to explore? How might you go about pursuing one or two of them?
2. Engage honestly with your student about the pros and cons of taking a gap year. How do they feel about taking a different path from their peers knowing that they will be a year or more longer in getting their degree.
3. Determine what you are willing to contribute toward the costs of your young adult's gap year and communicate your expectations regarding their time away.
4. Consider how supportive you are of losing non-refundable deposits should your young adult change their mind and not attend the college they had committed to. They don't have to apply to college and then defer. They could apply to college during their gap year which reduces stress in high school.
5. Get acquainted with the specific requirements including timeline for the deferral process and help your young adult craft and submit a plan for consideration.

Notes

Am I Too Late?

Chapter 6
Having a Walkabout

Please think about this as you go on.
 Breathe on the world.
Hold out your hands to it. When morning
 and evenings
roll along, watch how they open and close,
 how they
invite you to the long party that your life is.

—William Stafford

When our two sons were five and seven years old, we decided to make a major change in our life. Mike had been working at the same company for 16 years and was feeling really stuck and unhappy. My background in career and life coaching had not been helpful. I had encouraged him to quit and try something different but fear kept him from making a change. He felt the responsibility of being the full-time breadwinner and was afraid of moving on.

I worked hard to support Mike but was dealing with my own fears. Our youngest son, Stuart, had been born full-term weighing 3 lbs 14 ounces and had required a lot of my attention. Before he was born, I had been working as a part-time consultant but planned to pursue full-time work when Stuart began pre-school. I thought by providing more income that it would help Mike make a change.

Unfortunately, due to Stuart's special needs, my ability to work was limited. After multiple consults with different doctors and numerous tests, we finally received a diagnosis that Stuart had a rare genetic disorder, Russell-Silver Syndrome. Fortunately, it was not life-threatening, but it would require a specific treatment protocol to address his growth issues which included developmental delays.

When parents have children with special needs, it often leads to a great deal of stress and puts strain on the family. This was true for Mike and me. To deal with the challenges we were facing as a couple and as a family, we sought counseling. We were fortunate to be referred to a family therapist who used a systems approach in working with his clients. He challenged us to think of the choices we were making and what alternatives we might consider if we removed any fear for pursuing different options.

Reframing fear is an activity that I often use in my career and life coaching work with clients, so I was a little chagrined to realize that I had not sought to do this on my own!

Our work with Dr. Gee led us to make a major change in our life in order to change the patterns of behavior that we had fallen into. We decided to mind map a new life for ourselves. We sat together with post it paper on our walls and made a bucket list of all the things we would like to do, experience or learn, if money were no object.

The result was a "walkabout" for Mike.

The term "walkabout" is an Australian term used to describe a rite of passage in aboriginal society for adolescent males, typically ages 10 to 16, who live in the wilderness for a period of time as they make the transition into manhood.

Mike's walkabout changed all our lives

Mike quit his job, we put our house up for sale, took Mackenzie and Stuart out of school, and went to Australia to live and travel for three months. When we returned to the US, Mike spent a couple of months in Colorado living at my cousin's condo and skiing while I lived in Florida with the boys on the Gulf Coast. They attended a Montessori school in Pensacola for the spring term while I conducted a national job search in higher education. The goal was for me to secure a full-time job while Mike would take some time to figure out what was next for him.

To finance our plan, we took out a loan against our house and used our savings. It was a huge risk. Part of our budget included paying for COBRA medical insurance for 18 months. We needed to continue our health insurance coverage as Stuart's medication cost over $4k each month. Insurance covered a majority of the costs except for a small co-pay. We also tapped our family to help us, not financially, but for providing short-term housing during this time.

Off to Australia!

The first person we called was my brother Dan in Australia. He was living on the Gold Coast south of Brisbane, and had been wanting family to come visit. When asked if he would mind having visitors, he said we could stay as long as we wanted. We stayed three months, as long as our tourist visas would allow. The first month in Australia, we explored the Queensland area where Dan lived—hiking in the rainforest, and

Australia walkabout

exploring Burleigh Heads and Brisbane. Australia's trails are rich sources of learning with interpretive signs and exhibits.

The second month, we rented a camper van and completed a 6,000 mile loop of Australia. We started at Burleigh Heads and traveled up the Gold Coast of Queensland to Whitsunday Islands and the Great Barrier Reef. We then headed west to the Northern Territory, and then south to visit Alice Springs and Uluru, the famous monolith. We continued south to Adelaide and caught a ferry to Kangaroo Island to see the sea lions and the South Ocean. From there we returned to the mainland and headed east following the Great Ocean Road to see the Twelve Apostles. We skirted Melbourne to the north and returned to Burleigh Heads. The third month, we rented a van and took a second shorter trip to visit Sydney and see the Blue Mountains.

Mackenzie at Uluru

We each got to do something from our bucket list. Mackenzie's wish was to visit Uluru in the Northern Territory. Stuart wanted to see the duck-billed platypus in the wild. I wanted to drive the Great Ocean Road and visit Sydney and see the famous Opera House. Mike wanted to scuba dive in the Great Barrier Reef. We got to do all these things, and it was wonderful to see and experience a different way of life.

But what about schooling for the boys during this time?

We tried for a couple of weeks to homeschool but gave up on the idea when we began traveling in the camper van. Too much bouncing! When the boys returned to the US after missing a fall semester of school, they did not appear to have fallen behind. There was so much learning that had occurred from their time in Australia. It reminded me of the wise words of Jeff Greenfield at the University School of Nashville, "Don't let school get in the way of learning."

One of the biggest lessons for Mackenzie and Stuart was for them to see their parents "walk out" to "walk on" to a different future.

Hello Nashville!

Mike's walkabout resulted in a major change for us; it led to a relocation to Tennessee and my work at Vanderbilt University, and Mike's pursuit of a PhD in Mechanical Engineering. After 25 years of not being in school, Mike decided that what he really wanted to do with his life was to get a PhD in Mechanical Engineering. He wanted to teach and perform engineering research in an academic setting.

Mike's PhD commencement

Mike's decision to get his doctoral degree modeled for Mackenzie and Stuart the value of continued education and the importance of taking a "walkabout" or self-funded sabbatical.

A cousin of the walkabout—the gap year

Once he had our support, Mackenzie shared his desire to take a gap year with his college counselor. She recommended that he still continue to apply to colleges of interest, which is considered a best practice for high school students thinking of or planning to take a gap year. It is easier for them to go through the college search and decision-making process while they are seniors in high school. Once they commit to the college they plan to attend, students submit a request to the college admissions office that they are seeking to defer enrollment for a year along with a plan for their gap year.

Heeding his counselor's advice, Mackenzie continued with the college application and decision process. When he committed to attending the University of Miami on May 1st, he did so with the idea that he would defer his start date for a year. In mid-May, Mackenzie contacted the University of Miami admissions office about his desire to defer. He was instructed to submit a "plan" for his gap year that would be used by the university to decide whether to grant his deferral request. The university was clear in its expectation that Mackenzie develop a "good" gap year plan. And we were just the parents to help him do this type of work!

We engaged in an approach similar to the one we had used in planning Mike's walkabout. On the same white board used for mapping out Mackenzie's college visits the year before, we brainstormed what might be included in his plan. We started by posing two questions, "What would you like to learn next year?" And "What activities would you like to engage in?" From there, Mackenzie developed a bucket list of activities that fell into categories of "structured learning," "volunteer," and "work."

I was thrilled to see how excited he was about the different possibilities. He identified over twenty-five different experiences that he would like to engage in or topics he would like to learn more about. The list included volunteering at Big Brothers Big Sisters in Nashville, interning at an environmental firm, learning to play golf, and working at a ski resort.

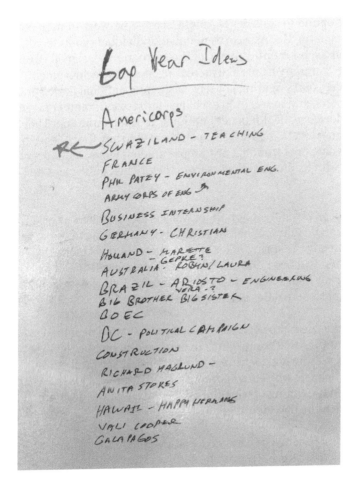

The infamous whiteboard for visualizing ideas

At this point, you may be wondering, what is the gap year going to cost. It was a concern for us as well. Mackenzie had heard of one program that a USN graduate ahead of him in school had done, and the cost was $30,000 for three months! The program had been primarily focused on volunteering in a small overseas community while living with a host family.

There are many excellent gap year programs available and a number are quite affordable. The Gap Year Association is an excellent resource if you are interested in researching gap year programs.

One free option to consider is AmeriCorps—a network of national service programs in the US. As a corps member, individuals volunteer between three and twelve months in one of three programs designed "to address critical community needs like increasing academic achievement, mentoring youth, fighting poverty, sustaining national parks, preparing for disasters, and more."[67] In exchange for service, volunteers receive a living allowance, health benefit options, and skills training. They also receive an education award that can be used to pay for college, graduate school, vocational training, or to repay student loans; and opportunities to work with leading employers from the private, public and non-profit sectors.

AmeriCorps was not an option for Mackenzie as he had missed the application deadline. When he seriously began to consider the gap year, it was already the spring of his senior year, and the AmeriCorps application had been due a few months before in the fall of his senior year. If your high school student is interested in this option, it is important to note dates when applications are due.

For Mackenzie's gap year, we decided that it would be more cost effective to use our personal connections in helping him pursue the experiences and activities he had identified as possibilities. We brainstormed a list of people we knew who could potentially help him with his gap year, and we discussed the timing of when he might engage in the different experiences he had identified.

The first experience he arranged was a volunteer teaching position in Swaziland for a spring term. The second experience he arranged was to live at his Aunt Mary Jo's condo in Colorado during the winter months with the goal of securing employment at a ski resort. Who wouldn't want to include this in a gap year—a built in opportunity to ski! All that remained for completing the "plan" was to figure out the "structured learning" experience that would occur during the fall.

Graduation came and went and Mackenzie had still not determined what he would be doing in the fall.

Finalizing the plan

His answer came in July when a good friend of ours, Kara Bingham, who had worked in higher education study abroad for many years, came for a visit. She recommended that Mackenzie look at a program through the National Outdoor Leadership School (NOLS). I had thought of NOLS earlier in our gap year discussions but had ruled it out because of cost. Mackenzie had a friend in high school who had participated in a NOLS summer program, and his mother had told me it had been transformative. When I went to the NOLS web site, however, and saw that tuition for an 80-day program would be approximately $14,000 (and that did not include equipment and travel costs), I did not suggest this option to Mackenzie. It was just too expensive.

Kara made the case, however, of what he would learn from the experience. She was an expert in experiential learning programs and knew the benefit that NOLS would provide him. She argued that the cost for the program was approximately equal to what we would have been paying for a semester at Miami, and she was correct. At the time, costs to attend the university were $62,000 for a year of tuition, room, and fees. Yikes! And that was 2015. We were not on the hook for this amount, thankfully.

Mackenzie was fortunate enough to benefit from my employment situation at Vanderbilt because it provided education benefits to dependents. Once we figured in the education benefit, income from scholarships and grants, and student employment, our tuition costs and expenses for Mackenzie to attend the University of Miami were projected to be $28,000 for the first year. We were on the hook for approximately $14,000 for each semester.

Kara said the only challenge that Mackenzie might have with the NOLS option was it might be too late to enroll in a fall program. It was already July. He quickly got online and researched options through NOLS. Luckily, he identified a couple of options that were still open for enrollment. He applied and was accepted to an 80-day NOLS course based in the Pacific Northwest. He agreed to pay half of the tuition costs from his college savings and we would pay the other half. Through the generosity of family in birthday and Christmas gifts over the years, and earnings from summer employment, Mackenzie had saved approximately $12K.

Mike and I agreed that it was a good investment of his college funds, knowing that his NOLS experience would be a defining time for him as he made the transition from high school to college. NOLS offered scholarships and Mackenzie thought about applying for one. However, based on his experience with college financial aid awards, he believed that our income would disqualify him, so decided not to apply.

In hindsight, I wish I had encouraged Mackenzie to apply for a scholarship. Organizations like NOLS seek to bring together individuals from diverse backgrounds. So if you are thinking that a NOLS program or a similar program is not an affordable option for your child's gap year, I recommend that you not be hasty in your assessment. There may very well be financial assistance available to reduce overall costs to you. Mackenzie learned later that a couple of his fellow NOLS participants paid approximately $1,000 in tuition for the course.

Our gap year plan

Once NOLS confirmed his enrollment, Mackenzie's gap year plan was set.

In August, he would fly to Seattle and begin his NOLS program. After completing the NOLS semester in November, he would fly from Seattle to Denver. He would then make his way to Silverthorne, Colorado located in Summit County, where he would live for the winter and work at one of the area ski resorts. In early January, he would return to Nashville for a couple of weeks before flying to Swaziland where he would volunteer at a school in Mbabane, the nation's capital, for three months. He would return to Nashville at the end of April and work for the summer before starting the University of Miami in August.

Overall, this was a well thought-out and structured gap year plan. Remember, Mackenzie needed to submit a plan that looked "good" for the University of Miami to approve his deferral for a year. It is important to note that a plan that would be approved by a college does not necessarily have to include travel and the activities that Mackenzie had included. If costs are an issue, there is value in a plan that includes staying at home, volunteering, and working.

Mackenzie's Gap Year Plan

August – November
- Fly to Seattle. Shuttle to NOLS Base Camp – Mt Vernon, WA.
- Complete NOLS 80-day Pacific Northwest Semester.
- Shuttle to Seattle airport.

November – January
- Fly to Denver. Shuttle to Aunt's Condo in Silverthorne.
- Get a job at ski resort in Summit County.
- Live at aunt's condo, work, + ski.
- Re-visit College Decision.
- Return to Nashville. Prepare for 3mos. Swaziland.

January – April
- Fly to Johannesburg, South Africa. Meet host family + travel by car to Mbabane, Swaziland.
- Volunteer at St. Marks High School for one term.
- Live with Inampasa family.
- Fly from Mbabane home to Nashville.

May – August
- Get a job in Nashville. Work | Save $ for college.
- Begin University of Miami

What You Can Do

1. Brainstorm a bucket list with your young adult about things they would like to learn about in their time away, and things they have always wanted to do but did not have the time to do.
2. Identify individuals in your network who could help your student develop their own opportunities to explore, learn, and create.
3. Encourage your student to research gap year programs and identify opportunities that fit within your budget. It doesn't hurt for you to research options in parallel so you can be informed or be in a position to suggest options to your student.

Notes

Currumbin Wildlife
Sanctuary

Australia Zoo

Kata Tjuta - Northern Territory

Am I Too Late?

Chapter 7
The Four Agreements

Too much caution is bad for you. By avoiding things you fear, you may let yourself in for unhappy consequences. It is usually wiser to stand up to a scary-seeming experience and walk right into it, risking the bruises and hard knocks. You are likely to find it is not as tough as you had thought. Or you may find it plenty tough, but also discover you have what it takes to handle it.

—Norman Vincent Peale

As an infant and in his early years, Mackenzie loved being outdoors. Mike and I would often tuck him into our Kelty backpack and head out the door for a hike in the mountains behind our house. We lived in the foothills of Pikes Peak in Colorado Springs with nature right outside our

Hiking - the easy way

back door. As he got older, Mackenzie would often engage in free-play on the deck or in the driveway next to tall pine trees and Aspen groves.

When he started Montessori school, Mackenzie had the opportunity to be outside several times a day and benefitted greatly from the Montessori approach of experiential education taught through the senses in the natural world.

Time in nature lessened after our move to Tennessee, when I returned to work full-time and Mike began his full-time PhD program. Organized sports, longer school days, increased homework, daily commutes, and weekends used for catching up on chores impacted the amount of time we spent outdoors individually or as a family. Hikes like we used to take when we lived in Colorado all but disappeared, as our sons transitioned from elementary to middle school and from middle school to high school. With finances being tight, we rarely took a vacation and, if we did, it involved visiting family.

Loving the outdoors

The impact on Mackenzie's overall well-being was significant. USN integrated naturalist and outdoor education into the school year, but it was limited to a week-long outdoor experience once a year. Mackenzie recognized that he needed something different but was not sure what that might be—a different school, maybe.

When he was a freshman at USN, Mackenzie brought home information on the Outdoor Academy—an outdoor school that USN had an agreement with where he could attend for a semester or year during his sophomore or junior year. He was really excited about the opportunity. I confess that I chose not to engage in a serious conversation with him about the school. All I could see were the costs. Tuition we were paying to USN would have covered most of the costs for the school, but not all. I just could not see where we could find the funds to cover the difference.

It was a missed opportunity that I later regretted as Mackenzie continued with the grind of high school, particularly when I saw the degree of anxiety and stress he was experiencing during his college search.

Twice he explored the idea of leaving USN to attend public high school, but ultimately made the decision to stay.

Reflecting on Mackenzie's high school years, I believe that he was experiencing nature deficit disorder. What's that?

In his groundbreaking book, *Last Child in the Woods: Saving Our Children From Nature-Deficit Disorder*, author Richard Louv concludes that direct exposure to nature is essential for healthy childhood development and for the physical and emotional health of children and adults.[68] He argues that our children's decreased exposure to nature in the US today has led to a "nature-deficit disorder." This involves "diminished use of senses, attention difficulties, and higher rates of physical and emotional illnesses." Louv highlights Michael Gurian's research that neurologically our brains have not caught up with today's overstimulating environment. "Getting kids out in nature can make a difference."

"Nature—the sublime, the harsh, and the beautiful," Louv writes,"offers something that the street or gated community or computer cannot. Nature presents the young with something so much greater than they are; it offers an environment where they can easily contemplate infinity and eternity...Immersion in the natural environment cuts to the chase, exposes the young directly and immediately to the very elements from which humans evolved: earth, water, air, and other living kin, large and small. Without that experience...we forget our place; we forget that larger fabric on which our lives depend."

Mackenzie needed nature to regain that sense of wholeness and interest in the world around him.

I often found myself wondering during Mackenzie's senior year, "Am I too late?" Was there something I could do to help him regain a sense of self, confidence in his choices, and re-engage his love for learning?

A semester course through the National Outdoor Leadership School (NOLS) became part of the solution. It was one of the three activities that Mackenzie would integrate as part of his learning journey (aka gap year).

The value of outdoor programs has been documented over the years. One particular study was highlighted by Louv. As part of research on attention and directed-attention fatigue, Stephen and Rachel Kaplan conducted a nine-year study for the US Forest Service that involved following participants in a wilderness program for up to two weeks. During the program and afterwards, participants reported "...experiencing a sense of peace and an ability to think more clearly; they also reported that just being in nature was more restorative than the physically challenging activities, such as rock climbing, for which such programs are mainly known."

Louv also shared findings from a comprehensive study by Yale University professor Stephen Kellert, who studied the long-term effects on teens who participated in one of three well-established wilderness-based education programs: the Student Conservation Association, the National Outdoor Leadership School, and Outward Bound. Positive results persisted through many years. Participants who depended on working with others reflected skills for enhanced cooperation, tolerance, compassion, intimacy, and friendship.

NOLS Fall Semester in the Pacific Northwest

Once Mackenzie made the decision to apply to and was accepted into the NOLS Fall Semester in the Pacific Northwest, it completed his "gap year" plan. I knew little about wilderness-based education programs and I was curious to see what the outcomes would be for him. Mackenzie would be living in an area of the US he had never visited before and participating in a course where the classroom would be outdoors in the North Cascade mountains and the waters of British Columbia.

NOLS offered the option of receiving 16 hours of college credit for the course but Mackenzie decided against it. This was mainly due to the restrictions from the University of Miami that prevented him from receiving academic credit from another institution while deferring enrollment for a year.

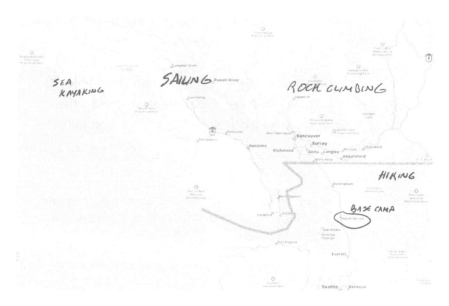

Pacific Northwest NOLS expedition

Experiential learning and leadership

At this point, you may be wondering about NOLS. Until Mackenzie decided to participate in a course, I did not know much about the school.

The National Outdoor Leadership School (more commonly known as NOLS) was founded in 1965 in Wyoming as a non-profit organization with the goal of teaching outdoor skills and leadership in the wilderness.[69] It has evolved over the past fifty years, helping create the US Leave No Trace Program, adopting an outcome-based education model, offering wilderness medicine training through its Wilderness Medicine Institute, partnering with colleges and universities to provide academic credit for NOLS programs, and offering professional training to corporate and institutional clients, including NASA.

NOLS' success is attributed to its outstanding leadership curriculum. It has created a framework defining ideal leadership characteristics and works to develop these skills in each individual participant engaged in a group cohort experience—often through a remote, back-country expedition. Students develop technical skills and learn how to lead and follow in a team.

NOLS fundamental philosophy is that leadership can be learned—even by those who don't think they have a natural ability to lead. The key is practice.

In a 2012 *Harvard Business Review* article by John Kanengieter and Aparna Rajagopal-Durbin, NOLS leadership training is described in practice. Through the "...unpredictable, challenging, and dynamic wilderness environment, our participants learn five key principles— *practice leadership, lead from everywhere, behave well, keep calm,* and *disconnect to connect.*"[70]

NOLS uses an experiential learning model developed by Case Western University's Weatherhead School of Management professor, David Kolb. The strategy is to give individuals who participate in expeditions "...more responsibility each day so they become comfortable making decisions, acting upon them, and reflecting on their outcomes." They develop an understanding of "consequential" leadership that includes learning how to fail.

As the co-founder of Netflix and a NOLS graduate, Marc Randolph describes in the 2012 *Harvard Business Review* article, "On a hike, it's a constant process of not being sure, taking a shot, and finding out one, 10, or 100 minutes later whether your decision was a good or bad one...

That's what you face in the business world, especially as an entrepreneur...Making decisions on the basis of incomplete, inconclusive, or contradictory information is a skill that managers at every level must master."

In addition to practicing leadership, NOLS participants learn how to "lead from everywhere." They are taught to lead in one of "...four ways during an expedition and to take different approaches depending on the circumstances." The four roles of leadership are designated leadership, active followership, peer leadership, and self leadership. "The *designated leader* takes responsibility for the group and determines how it will achieve its goals. That person is supported by *active followers*, who participate in group decision-making by seeking clarity and giving input. All team members are encouraged to be *peer leaders*, taking action to help one another. They are also expected to exercise *self-leadership* by being organized and motivated and by caring for themselves so that they can effectively take on the other three roles."

As they practice different leadership roles, participants are provided feedback by their instructors and peers on different leadership skills. These include expedition behavior, vision and action, communication, judgement and decision-making, self-awareness, tolerance for adversity, and competence.

In my experience working with students in higher education, I have never seen such an effective leadership training model in preparing individuals for the workplace and for life in general. By the end of a NOLS course, participants have gained skills in self-reliance, judgment, risk management, and the confidence to thrive when faced with uncertainty. They also possess an ability to accept feedback from others and give feedback in a positive, constructive manner; skills many young adults lack when they graduate from college.

Some NOLS graduates who have been successful in the business world that you may recognize include: Marc Randolph, Cofounder of Netflix; Lesley Mottla, Executive VP at Zipcar; Peter Roy, Founder of Whole Foods Market; Perry Klebahn, Former CEO of Timbuk2; and John Grunsfeld, Retired NASA astronaut and Chief Scientist.

Who wants some fear and uncertainty?

In August, Mike and I saw Mackenzie off at the airport in Nashville. He was flying to Seattle, where he would take a shuttle to NOLS base camp located in Mt. Vernon, Washington. Mackenzie's backpack was "stuffed" with the supplies that NOLS had suggested he bring for his outdoor semester in the Pacific Northwest. Many of his friends had headed off to college by this time and, like them, Mackenzie was excited about the adventure that lay ahead for the semester.

He texted us a couple of times before he reached base camp—once when he landed and was waiting for his shuttle, and the second time to let us know that he was on the shuttle headed to Mt. Vernon. He shared that there were a couple of individuals on the shuttle with him who were also participating in the same NOLS course.

At this point, we did not know how often we would hear from Mackenzie, since much of the time he would be in the back country with limited access to cell service and the Internet. NOLS also asked students to refrain from cell phone use while on expeditions in order for them to be fully immersed in the outdoor experience. The focus was on becoming "technology-free" during this time.

Over the next 80 days, Mackenzie would FaceTime us periodically when he returned to base camp and had Internet access. We learned that he was part of a group of nine students with two instructors. As the group was introduced to the different technical skills of the course, the instructors would change.

Mackenzie discovered that he was the youngest member of the group, being 18; the oldest student was Tara, age 24. She had not been to college and was working as a bartender prior to enrolling in the NOLS course. Another student had started college but dropped out and had no plans to go back. The other six students had each started college but had decided to take a gap semester or year for a number of reasons. All were looking for a transformative learning experience.

The first section of the fall semester course began with a 19-day sea kayak expedition in Nootka Sound on Vancouver Island led by two instructors. On the way to Tahsis, British Columbia, where the expedition would launch, the group met with a First Nations' wood carver and were introduced to the natural and cultural history of the area. The group paddled over 150 nautical miles during their kayak expedition. Along the way, they learned about maneuvering sea kayaks, pod travel, camp set-up, cooking skills, leadership theory, communication, navigation, food rationing, and adjusting plans due to unsafe conditions resulting from inclement weather.

The group was also introduced to the Environmental Studies curriculum embedded in the 80-day course which included regional plant identification and sustainable agriculture. The curriculum was similar to what one might find in an Environmental Studies classroom but enhanced by the hands-on, experiential nature of the program.

Sea kayaking - am I having fun?

After 3 ½ weeks of sea kayaking, the group returned to base camp to prepare for its next segment, rock climbing. Mackenzie took advantage of WiFi to check in with us. He shared that the sea kayaking had been a difficult experience; a number of students had wanted to quit early on because it was so physically demanding. The rainy days had made it even more difficult, and setting up camp after paddling much of the day was not "fun." He said that the first time he set up his tent, it took him over an hour, and he had been "really" frustrated that something this simple was so difficult in the beginning. He also said that it was almost the end of their 3 ½ weeks on the water before he had finally gotten the hang of paddling.

Every evening, the group would prepare their dinner and take the opportunity to discuss the day, facilitated by their instructor. They reflected on lessons learned, environmental topics including ethics and philosophy, and were introduced to leadership concepts. Despite the initial feeling of wanting to quit, all the participants had come together as a cohesive group and the experience had been positive and rewarding. Mackenzie said that he did not "love" sea kayaking but was proud that he had acquired the skills through determination and willingness to tough it out.

The next part of the course was focused on building technical skills of rock climbing. Several of the students had previous climbing experience, but Mackenzie had climbed only once as part of a high school outdoor trip. The 17-day rock climbing section of the course took place in Squamish, British Columbia, with base camp at Paradise Valley campground and daily trips to various technical climbing crags. The climbing curriculum focused on a solid foundation of technical climbing skills including belaying and climbing movement, basic knots and rope skills, anchor building, top rope site management, artificial protection placement, lead climbing theory and practice, rock climbing risk management, rappelling, basic rescue techniques, and an introduction to multi-pitch climbing.

The leadership curriculum focused on developing self-awareness and working toward ambitious goals in an organized and deliberate way to track progress and celebrate successes. There was a strong emphasis on environmental studies during this course including participation in a community shoreline clean-up and a visit to a local organic farm to learn more about how the six ecological concepts and the system of a circular economy are at work in small-scale organic farming. The group also learned how to plan and budget for groceries—a very important life skill.

When he checked in with us after completing the rock-climbing segment of the course, Mackenzie was really pumped. He had fallen in love with the physicality and focus required of him. He also shared that during this segment some conflict had arisen between several members of the group, with one person saying negative and hurtful comments about another individual in the group. This concerned Mackenzie and a fellow student when they saw the behavior and its impact on the group. They felt that

The thrill of the climb

they needed to address it, especially since they would be living together for the next 60 days. Mackenzie and the other student shared their observations and facilitated a group meeting on conflict resolution. People were able to share their feelings and different backgrounds, and tried to meet each where they were at. It had been a difficult conversation for Mackenzie and the others, but worth it. The behavior changed after the feedback had been shared, and the dynamic of the group was much healthier throughout the rest of the course.

When Mackenzie shared this experience with us, I was amazed at the level of maturity and confidence that he had acquired in order to provide feedback to his peers. He typically sought approval from his peers often going along with the status quo. I was particularly impressed with the focus on feedback and the trust that had been established to create a safe space for these conversations to occur.

Embracing the work of Don Miguel Ruiz

In addition to acquiring rock climbing skills, the group informally explored the philosophical work of Don Miguel Ruiz, *The Four Agreements*. Throughout the course, members of the group would share books they were reading and discuss as a group, enriching the learning experience. *The Four Agreements* was one of the books that had been discussed and Mackenzie had found it inspirational. He encouraged Mike and I to read the book. He said it had really helped him think about his life in a different way and was excited about discussing it with us.

So why did this book have such a profound impact on him?

After reading it, I understood.

In *The Four Agreements*, author Don Miguel Ruiz offers a code of conduct based on ancient Toltec wisdom that advocates freedom from self-limiting beliefs for us to realize our full potential as well-balanced and happy people.

Ruiz believes that "...everything a person does is based on agreements they have made with themselves, with others, with God, and with life itself." Unfortunately, society and the outside world has defined how we "should" behave, which results in self-limiting beliefs based on fear. "We are told what's acceptable, what's not acceptable, and we are taught to judge." Our behavior is based on operant conditioning, argues Ruiz. "When you are bad and flaunt the rules, you will be punished. When you obey, you will get a reward. The reward is subtly pernicious because it teaches us to act for the reward itself instead of finding pleasure in the action. The fear of punishment instead becomes the fear of not being good enough. And with both punishment and rewards, we learn to wear a mask to please others."

According to Ruiz, to be happy, we must rid ourselves "...of society-imposed and fear-based agreements that may subconsciously influence our behavior and mindset. *The Four Agreements* shows us that there is a different way. By breaking free from the societal structures and expectations, we can make new agreements for ourselves."

When I read the book, I was struck by both the simplicity of the words and the power of the ideas behind the message. My son had become my teacher.

The Four Agreements

1. **Be Impeccable With Your Word**
2. **Don't Take Anything Personally**
3. **Don't Make Assumptions**
4. **Always Do Your Best**

I was also impressed that Mackenzie had gained insight into how he could address the fear of "not being good enough" and found a way to change self-limiting beliefs. In my career and life coaching work, self-limiting beliefs are one of the biggest challenges individuals face as they seek to make change throughout their adult lives. The fact that my 18-year-old son had gained insight into ways to address this challenge was extremely positive. I felt it would give him an edge as he navigated his launch into adulthood.

In addition to personal books such as *The Four Agreements* that members of the group shared, instructors carried books for students to read and discuss. Students also gave presentations on a book of their choice. Mackenzie chose one focused on the spotted owl and the multiple viewpoints of logging in the Pacific Northwest. Additionally, instructors carried a packet of readings, ranging from environmental philosophy to inspirational quotes to stories, that were shared and discussed as a group.

I recognized the value of these informal and formal discussions on different topics throughout the NOLS course. Mackenzie and other members of his cohort could apply what they learned in everyday life as members of the group. The different texts they read and shared provided a context for the outdoor group experiences and deep learning occurred. If he had read these books and texts as part of a traditional academic class in college, I believe the outcome would have been far less impactful.

The next time we spoke to Mackenzie, he was back at base camp after finishing a segment on Wilderness First Aid and an 18-day mountain hiking expedition. The group hiked 115 miles through the Pacific Northwest Mountains, starting at North Cascades National Park and finishing at the Pasayten Wilderness. The focus during this segment was on developing solid outdoor skills to ensure the ability to survive in the wilderness in different weather conditions including rain, hail, cold, and heat. One of the highlights for Mackenzie during this segment was the opportunity to complete a multi-day hike with two other students without instructors, testing his ability to face different challenges that arose due to the terrain and weather.

Navigating the waters of British Columbia

The last segment of the fall semester course found the group learning seamanship skills by sailing 226 nautical miles on the Salish Sea from Campbell River to Nanaimo, British Columbia, on two 36' sailboats. Their challenges included navigating large crossings of the Strait of Georgia, timing tidal currents through Beasley Passage and Hole in the Wall, and coastal piloting through Desolation Sound. In addition to seamanship, students worked with their peers to lead and facilitate group discussions on resource issues—food and water, trash and recycling, compost and humanure, and fossil fuels—and used an environmental studies journal to track their observations and note their reflections on the natural world.

When Mackenzie returned to base camp after completing the sailing segment of the course, he once again checked-in with us by FaceTime. He had fallen in love with sailing and was extremely proud of what he had learned and was confident in his abilities. He said the group had grown incredibly close over the semester and were sad that the course was ending and that they would all be going their separate ways. Before flying to Denver where he would meet us at the airport, Mackenzie shared that he had arranged to spend a couple of days exploring Seattle with two of his NOLS friends. He was excited to see another city that he had not visited before.

I wondered what changes we would see when we saw him in a few days. From my perspective, NOLS had been a powerful learning experience for Mackenzie, and the immersion in nature with time for reflection had been transformative.

What You Can Do

1. Discuss the frequency of communication that you seek to have with your young adult if they plan to not live with you during their time away.
2. Affirm your support for your young adult to be independent.
3. Explore the concept of curiosity with your young adult and reflect on times they have exhibited this in their life.

Notes

NOLS - learning by doing

Am I Too Late?

Chapter 8
Don't Let School Get in the Way of Learning

How we use our privileges and opportunities defines what kind of person we are.

—Priya Haji

Gap year proponents say that a "good" gap year plan includes time for "working." Not volunteering, but actually working at a job for pay. Any job—customer service, manual labor, retail, hospitality.

A Forbes article cited Pew Research revealing that "today's young adults (between the ages of 15-21) are much less likely to have had a paid summer job or to have been employed last year compared to every previous generation for which data exists." [71]

More than half (58%) of 16 to 19-year-olds had a paid summer job in 1978 compared 35% who had one in 2017 and the number of 15 to 17-year-olds who reported having any type of work dropped from 48% in 1968 to 19% in 2018.

What?!!!

It's not hard to connect the dots between employers who say college graduates aren't prepared for the work force and graduates who have had little to no work experience and little understanding of what it takes to earn a paycheck.

When I was a Vanderbilt, it was not uncommon to see students with no work experience coming into the Career Center for help with their resume. Not even a summer job. This is not unique to Vanderbilt.

Many young adults entering college have been too busy to work during the summer because their parents have signed them up for activities that would help them be competitive for college admissions: debate camp, track camp, SAT/ACT prep, unpaid internship, etc. If they do work, it is not typically an unskilled job like janitorial work, but rather an office job working for a relative or friend of their parents.

As you may recall, for Mackenzie's gap year, he had planned to get a job at a ski area in Colorado when he finished his NOLS course in November. He did not care what kind of job, but was hoping to get a ski pass as part of working at the ski area. He was not incorrect in his thinking because part of the pay for employees working at ski areas for a season typically includes a season ski pass. Mackenzie knew he would have about two months to ski (and, yes, of course work!) before returning to Nashville to prepare for his departure for Swaziland in late January.

To help with affordability, because, as you can guess, it is expensive to live and work in a ski area, Mackenzie's aunt had generously offered to let him stay at her ski condo in Silverthorne. She would not charge him rent or utilities, and it was fairly convenient to a bus stop. Mackenzie would not have a car while he was in Colorado so he planned to utilize Summit County's public transportation to get around the area and to work. "Fairly" convenient meant it would be a half-mile hike in the snow. For a strong young 18-year-old athlete, no problem!

The original plan had Mackenzie taking a shuttle to the ski condo from Denver airport. However, Mike and I decided to fly to Denver and meet him. Like most parents of college-age children, we were looking forward to his homecoming after three months of "school." We were eager to see him and hear about his NOLS experience in the Pacific Northwest. It would be two more months before he would return to Nashville, so we decided to welcome him home in Colorado! After living in the state for 16 years, it felt like home. We also could help him with some food supplies for his two-month stay. What are parents for, right?!?!

I was particularly eager to see him in-person after having just monthly FaceTime calls from NOLS base camp. I wanted to be reassured about his health and safety.

The reunion

At my first sight of Mackenzie coming through airport security into the main terminal at DIA, I thought to myself, "Oh my! Who is this young man walking toward me with the long hair, scruffy beard, backpack, and huge smile on his face?"

"Hi Mom! Hi Dad!" Mackenzie said as he hugged both of us enthusiastically. "Thanks for picking me up. It's great to see you!"

As I hugged my son, I was overwhelmed with love. "It's great to see you too!" I could not believe how good he looked.

My next thought was "Wow! He really stinks!" Spending time in the backcountry where bathing was infrequent, Mackenzie's body, clothes and backpack were particularly pungent. "Could be a long two-hour drive to the condo," I thought to myself.

Mom's buying dinner!

I had my son back!

Over the next three days, I was thrilled with the changes that I saw in Mackenzie. He was engaged, active in conversations, interested in learning, and appeared grounded from his time outdoors. He was also excited about his next venture—to secure a job at a ski resort and, of course, ski!

With a little help from me (after all, it is nice to have a Mom as a career coach, right?!), Mackenzie's resume was updated and he was ready to apply for jobs.

The good news? Resort areas need lots of employees during peak season, so finding a job was not difficult. Mackenzie read in the local newspaper that Keystone Resort was hosting a job fair. He went to the fair, completed an application, and was hired on the spot to work at Keystone Mountain Lodge and Food Court—a Vail Resorts property. Amazingly good luck! That and the fact that he had prior work experience.

Mackenzie had worked at the Vanderbilt University Recreation Center every summer since he was sixteen as a lifeguard, camp counselor, and swim instructor. You've got to love the fact that the school swimming he had been involved with for many years led to his working for three summers at a pool for pay!

Mackenzie acquired a number of valuable skills while working at the Recreation Center, including "how to show up" to work, instructing children of different ages, working with others as part of a team, communicating with his supervisor, and safety and risk management.

Having previous work experience definitely helped Mackenzie get a job at Keystone. Once he started work, his supervisor recognized his ability to adapt to different roles quickly. As a result, he had the opportunity to learn many things including how to operate a snowblower, perform janitorial work, run a cash register, train new employees, act as a barista, and open and close the food court.

Using the 'woo'

What helped Mackenzie get a job offer on the spot at the job fair and also be successful at Keystone was his ability to leverage his strengths: woo, adaptability, activator, relator, and communication.

So what do I mean by "leverage his strengths?"

During the infamous spring break road trip that involved college visits during Mackenzie's junior year at USN, I thought it would be fun to have Mackenzie and Stuart take the Clifton StrengthsFinder—an online assessment developed by Gallup Education based on the work of Donald Clifton. We had begun using the assessment at Vanderbilt as part of a widespread movement happening at colleges and universities across the US to help students identify their strengths and talents. This information was particularly helpful in career counseling and academic advising. A number of colleges had moved to using a "strengths-based" approach as part of their campus-wide student success strategy.

To understand Mackenzie's "woo" (winning others over), it may be helpful to know the relationship between strengths and talents. For example, Mackenzie has a talent of being drawn to strangers and enjoys the challenge of making a connection with them. He has a strength in this area, because he consistently builds networks of supporters who know him and are prepared to help him.[72]

Mackenzie's top five Signature Themes (strengths)

1. **Adaptability: living in the moment, flexible**
2. **Woo: winning others over**
3. **Activator: action is best device for learning**
4. **Relater: derive pleasure and strength from close friends**
5. **Communication: use words to pique interest, inspire others to act**

When an individual takes the assessment, the 34 themes (strengths) are rank-ordered with the top five being the most relevant. The results help an individual understand their unique way of accomplishing their goals by building relationships, thinking strategically, executing plans, and influencing others.[73]

Within a couple of weeks, Mackenzie was tapped to be the Lead Cashier, a position which involved training individuals much older than he was, many whose English was their second language. Keystone, like other ski resorts, hired a number of international students seeking to work in the US and provided them with subsidized housing, board, and a small living stipend. As a result, Mackenzie had the opportunity to work with individuals from different cultures and backgrounds and experience a multicultural work environment—a critical competency for today's global workplace.

He also became friends with a number of his work colleagues. From short order cooks to lift operators, their life stories were often a stark contrast to Mackenzie's privileged background. He would not have gained this experience by attending a private college like the University of Miami.

Learning outside the classroom

Working and spending time with older adults also came with inherent risks. Because a number of employees lived in subsidized housing offered by the ski resort, it resulted in a "party-like" communal housing situation similar to college dorms but with a much more international resident base. Many of Mackenzie's work colleagues that he spent time with outside work were from countries where the legal drinking age was 16. Their relationship with alcohol and drugs, however, was much more measured than what is found at US colleges and universities. These adults did not begin drinking on Thursday evenings and continue thru Sunday only to sober up in time for Monday classes. These adults might have a couple of drinks or share a joint during the week or over the weekend. I was not naive enough to believe that Mackenzie would forgo these activities, but felt that it was better he engage in this behavior with mature adults than with college peers who drink to excess and engage in risky behaviors.

Mackenzie learned other lessons while working for Vail Resorts including the issue of affordable housing. Hourly workers could not afford the housing costs in Summit County, so Vail Resorts built dorm-like facilities and provided housing to its employees at a reduced rate. Employees paid monthly rent and typically lived in a double with another employee.

In Mackenzie's first month, he observed firsthand the power of employees coming together to advocate for their rights. Vail Resorts had decided to increase the number of employees living in one room to three and even four individuals who shared the same space. Employees, however, were being charged the single-occupancy rate rather than receiving a reduced rate. As you can imagine, the company's decision was unpopular, and employees demanded action to improve their living conditions.

I was blown away by what Mackenzie learned from this experience. At 18, I would have never had the opportunity to sit in a company-wide meeting with the Vice President of Human Resources in order to discuss employee concerns and possible solutions. Mackenzie did, and by doing so, received an education in employee rights, fair housing laws, and corporate responsibility. This learning occurred in-person and not in a classroom.

A little fun to go with work

For the first time in his life, Mackenzie was living on his own and responsible for all his expenses except for rent and utilities. He was particularly struck by the costs for food—whether it was buying groceries or what people paid for lunch at the ski area. He told us, after working at the cash register at the ski resort's food court, he understood why Mike and I packed lunches when we skied.

One day, three boys in their early teens came to check out at his cash register and realized that they did not have enough cash to pay for their meals. The total cost for the three of them was over $60. One of the boys called his mother so she could provide a credit card number for Mackenzie to use to cover their meal. He said he recognized how privileged these boys were and thought the parent should not have bailed them out. He had learned something from this moment. He had seen himself in these boys and realized that he was thankful for the times that Mike and I had said "no" when he pleaded with us to buy food from the grill. Being on his feet all day working at the food court, Mackenzie had developed an understanding of the effort it took to earn a dollar and the importance of making spending decisions within a budget.

In December, Mike, Stuart, and I joined Mackenzie for the winter holidays in Colorado. Stuart had not seen his brother for almost five months and was eager to spend time with him when he was not working. We were all excited to ski. It had been a few years since we had last had the opportunity.

December was also the month that Mackenzie had planned to revisit his college decision to attend the University of Miami. He needed to resubmit financial aid information and check in with the university since he had deferred enrollment, and see what steps he needed to take to be starting in the fall. Due to his NOLS and Keystone experiences, however, Mackenzie was not 100% sure he wanted to attend Miami. It no longer seemed to be a good fit, but if he did not go there, where would he go?

What about college?

At this point, Mackenzie had completed only one-third of his gap year plan, and I felt he was not ready or prepared to make a final decision about attending the University of Miami. I believed taking more time and experiencing more of life outside the education bubble would provide him perspective. After all, January would find him heading to Swaziland for three months of volunteering, which could influence his thinking about his college choice.

At Mackenzie's request, we sat down together one evening with the sole purpose of discussing his college plans. When he began to start talking about college again, it was almost deja vu from his senior year. Gone was the centered individual that had returned from NOLS. Rubbing his hand back and forth across his forehead, Mackenzie indicated his stress. After observing this behavior, Mike asked him a very important question.

"If you did not go to the University of Miami next year, what would you see yourself doing?"

Without hesitation, Mackenzie responded. "I would thru hike the Appalachian Trail (AT). I would begin in the summer and end sometime in the fall."

"How long would it take you?" I asked.

"Probably about five months," he replied.

"How much would it cost?" I asked.

Mackenzie replied, "Anywhere between $2400-$3000 depending on equipment that I would need to buy. This would cover my travel expenses and supplies."

"Do you have the funds to cover this?" I asked.

"Yes, I do." Mackenzie responded. "I also could work for a couple of months when I get back from Swaziland to earn some money."

"Then it seems like you know what you want to do, Mackenzie. Why not do it?"

Mike agreed.

Mackenzie just sat there on the couch and looked at the two of us in amazement. His face lit up with joy. "You are the best parents! Not every parent would agree with you."

Hiking the Appalachian Trail?

From the conversation, it was evident that Mackenzie had been thinking for quite some time about thru-hiking the AT but had not given himself permission to take action around the idea. For those of you unfamiliar with the AT, like I was, the AT is a 2,200 mile hiking trail on the east coast, and people attempt to "thru-hike" the trail by hiking its entire length in a single year.

To my way of thinking, Mackenzie had no debt and no commitments to worry about, so taking five to six months of his life to hike the AT made sense from a timing perspective. He was only 18. Once he got involved with college, graduated, and began work, it would be much harder for him to take that length of time off for a long-distance hike. One more year of deferring college would not make a difference in the long run compared to the learning that would occur from hiking the AT.

Remember: Don't let school get in the way of learning.

Mackenzie decided that he would not make a final decision about attending the University of Miami or his other option of hiking the AT until he returned from Swaziland at the end of April. He planned to move forward with contacting the university's Admissions and Financial Aid Offices to confirm next steps should he decide to enroll for the Fall Term.

With a plan in place (a flexible one at that!), Mackenzie was able to enjoy the time he had left in Colorado. He returned to Nashville the second week in January ready for his next learning journey—Swaziland.

Mackenzie's Gap Year Plan

August - November
- Fly to Seattle. Shuttle to NOLS Base Camp - Mt Vernon, WA.
- Complete NOLS 80-day Pacific Northwest Semester.
- Shuttle to Seattle airport.

November - January
- Fly to Denver. Shuttle (Mom + Dad) to Aunt's Condo in Silverthorne.
- Get a job at ski resort in Summit County.
- Live at aunt's condo, work, + ski.
- Re-visit College Decision.
- Return to Nashville. Prepare for 3mos. Swaziland.
  + Explore 2nd Gap Year - Hike AT

January - April
- Fly to Johannesburg, South Africa. Meet host family + travel by car to Mbabane, Swaziland.
- Volunteer at St. Marks High School for one term.
- Live with Incumpusa family.
- Fly from Mbabane home to Nashville.

May - August
- Get a job in Nashville. Work / Save $ for college.
- Begin University of Miami

What You Can Do

1. Engage your young adult in a conversation about the jobs and volunteer work they have had so far. What did they like and dislike? What did they learn? Would they do them again?
2. Discuss with your young adult about the life they want to live and how work might support them.
3. Think about your comfort level with taking risks and the impact on the choices you have made in life. Engage your young adult in a conversation about what you would consider to be acceptable risks.

Notes

Chapter 9
Swaziland Calling

A person born to be a flower pot will not go beyond the porch.
—Swaziland proverb

You can't make this stuff up.

We never imagined when we were creating the gap year plan that it would take Mackenzie to Swaziland where he would teach English to high school students.

Here's how it happened.

As you may recall, a "good" gap year includes a time for service. One of the things on Mackenzie's bucket list for his gap year was to volunteer—at a school either in the US or internationally, or with a community-based organization. His interest stemmed from volunteer work during high school, when he volunteered as a mentor through the Big Brothers Big Sisters program and aided in one of the lower-level classrooms at USN. Mackenzie enjoyed working in a mentoring capacity and was drawn to the idea of volunteer work at a school during his gap year.

Working the network

Knowing that we could not afford a gap year program that would place Mackenzie as a volunteer in an international school or related educational setting, we chose to leverage our network. Brainstorming together, we identified several individuals who might be able to help. One of the individuals that made the most sense to contact was Peter Inampasa. At the time, he reported directly to the Minister of Education in Swaziland, so we thought he might be able to help arrange a volunteer opportunity for Mackenzie at a school in his hometown Mbabane. (Note: a year after Mackenzie left Swaziland, the King of Swaziland changed the name of the country to eSwatini. For the purpose of this book, I am going to use the country's former name of Swaziland because that was the name used when Mackenzie lived there).

We met Peter a few years before when he attended Peabody College of Education at Vanderbilt as a Fellow in the Hubert H. Humphrey Fellowship Program. The Fellowship was part of a Fulbright exchange program for educational leaders from developing countries. When I heard there was a need for host families for the university's first cohort, I volunteered. Mike and I had hosted several international students during my time working at Colorado College and loved the experience. We knew our time with Peter would be special when we met him the night the university welcomed the incoming Fellows to campus.

And it was.

A Few Facts About Swaziland

1. A country, slightly smaller than New Jersey, landlocked between South Africa and Mozambique.
2. Gained its independence from Britain in 1968.
3. Led by King MSWATI III - hereditary monarch.
4. Classified as a lower-middle income country but with high levels of poverty and high unemployment.
5. Population - 1,104, 479 (2020 est)
6. World's highest HIV/AIDS prevalence rate.
7. English and siSwati are official languages.

During Peter's year in the US, we had the opportunity to spend a great deal of time with him and we had become close. He did not live with us but we saw him regularly. All the Humphrey Fellows were housed in an apartment complex near campus. We also met his wife, Precious, and his son, Laston, when they came for a month visit midway through Peter's program. Because of our relationship, I felt comfortable emailing Peter and sharing with him Mackenzie's interest in volunteering and asking if he would be willing to help.

His response came almost immediately. He would love to help and offered for Mackenzie to live with him and his family should he come. At this point, I connected Mackenzie with Peter to work out details. Peter introduced Mackenzie to the Principal of St. Marks High School in Mbabane via email.

After a few emails were exchanged, it was agreed that Mackenzie would volunteer at St. Marks for the 2016 Spring Term, which began in late January and ended in late April. He would also coach track and swimming.

Mackenzie was now set! His international service experience was arranged and it looked to be affordable. The largest expense would be the roundtrip airline ticket from Nashville to Johannesburg, South Africa. Peter had generously offered to provide housing and food for Mackenzie. Of course, there would be a few incidental expenses to cover during his three months, but these would be minimal. Mike and I knew that the experience to live and work in another country would be invaluable for Mackenzie and that our investment in this alternative learning experience would be worth it.

Kind of like Study Abroad

Always thinking about return on investment (ROI), I compared our projected costs to what colleges charge for a study abroad experience and knew that we were paying far less for similar learning outcomes. Or, I would argue, improved learning outcomes. Mackenzie had arranged this volunteer opportunity on his own—being self-directed is a critical skill for adults. He also had to deal with the consequences when a few details were overlooked making arrangements for his volunteer role. What happened as a result was a richer learning experience for Mackenzie.

In mid-January, after having been gone for five months, Mackenzie returned to Nashville from Colorado. Preparing for his time in Swaziland was a whirlwind. Peter had told him that work attire would be formal. Quite a switch for him—going from back-packing and hiking gear in the fall to dress shoes, slacks, and sport coat in the spring. He was also encouraged to bring a suit to wear, as he would be attending church regularly with the family. Since Mackenzie's wardrobe did not include most of these things, we hit the secondhand clothing stores and Goodwill to purchase what he needed.

BNA to JNB

Time flew by, and in the last week of January Mike and I dropped Mackenzie off at the Nashville airport with his two suitcases in hand. He was ready to make the 30-hour trip to Johannesburg, where he would meet Peter.

Seeing him off, I was filled with excitement that he was heading toward an experience that would most likely be life-changing. I was also a little nervous about his traveling so far without phone service and with limited access to the Internet.

In our connected world today, this created some angst on my part. He was traveling a long way and his trip involved two airport transfers in different countries. If there were an issue, he would not have a way of communicating with us. I also worried that he would have difficulty connecting with Peter when he arrived in Johannesburg because he would not be able to call him upon arrival.

I reminded myself, however, that Mackenzie was very capable of dealing with crises, particularly, after his NOLS experience. He had previously traveled abroad so he was familiar with navigating issues associated with international travel. My concern was that he had never travelled that far by himself.

Despite telling myself that Mackenzie would be okay, I was very relieved when I received an email from Peter saying that Mackenzie had arrived safely. I was also glad to receive a second email from Peter when they arrived at Peter's home in Mbabane.

Peter's wonderful family

Mackenzie was welcomed into the household by Peter and his wife Precious, their 17-year-old son Laston and 8-year-old grandson Gabriel. As you might recall, Mackenzie had met both Precious and Laston when they visited Peter in Nashville, so they were not complete strangers. Gabriel would become Mackenzie's shadow during the three months; the two often played video games together and spent time just hanging out.

From the very beginning of his time in Swaziland to the end, the generosity of Peter and his family made Mackenzie's home stay in

Mbabane very special. They treated him like one of the family and not a guest. They worked to ensure that he felt comfortable as he acclimated to a different culture. Recognizing that Mackenzie might benefit from some privacy, Laston gave up his bedroom and moved in to share Gabriel's bedroom.

Peter and Precious Inampasa

Mackenzie's home stay was not necessarily typical of other students on gap years. Peter and Precious were both professionals, earned a good income, and lived in a nice home. In fact, they owned two other homes in Zambia. They would be considered "affluent" in Swazi terms.

Precious did all the cooking; however, she expected the "boys" to help with household chores. I was glad to hear that Mackenzie and Laston were assigned kitchen clean-up and dish duty after meals. Like many professional women in the US, the bulk of the household duties fell to Precious. She was quite busy as she taught full-time at Sifundzani School, one of the best schools in Swaziland, and also had two children to care for —Laston and Gabriel.

Peter was quite busy with his work at the Ministry of Education and Training Head Office as Senior Inspector of Schools where he was responsible for the French Language nationally. When we spent time with Peter in the US, we were impressed with his education and background. He spoke six languages fluently: French, English, his mother tongue Kaonde, and three Zambian languages - Bemba, Nyanja, and Tonga. He also understood other Zambian local languages. Peter had lived in Zambia, France, Sweden, and the US and had visited a number of European countries, and over 20 Middle Eastern and African countries. Because of this, Peter possessed a unique world view that Mackenzie was exposed to during his time in Mbabane.

As educators, Peter and Precious took time to share their knowledge with Mackenzie about Swaziland—present and past, the colonization of the various African countries, and about their own home country of Zambia. Precious had grown up in the Southern Province and Peter came from the North Western Province, though he had grown up and been educated in Lusaka, the capital city of Zambia. From his conversations with Peter and Precious, Mackenzie began to learn about the impact of colonization on African indigenous peoples. This profoundly shaped his worldview and he continued to seek to learn about colonialism back in the US.

Mackenzie also attended church with the family twice a week—on Wednesday evenings and most of the day on Saturdays. Peter, like a majority of Swazis, is a devout Christian, following Seventh Day Adventist teachings. We had not raised Mackenzie in a specific religious tradition so he found the experience enlightening—an introduction to spiritual life and what it meant to those who embraced formal religion. He said he fell in love with the music of the church.

Teaching English in a foreign country

After Mackenzie had spent a couple of days getting settled in Mbabane, Peter took him to the high school, introduced him to Principal Zwane, and left them to get acquainted.

At this point it was discovered that the email communications between Mackenzie and Principal Zwane had missed a few details, one being rather important—Mackenzie's age.

On first seeing Mackenzie, the principal expressed surprise at how young he was. She had been expecting someone much older—possibly retired and in their 50's. Not someone 18 and about the same age as the upper level learners in high school!

Mackenzie was also in for a surprise. What he thought would be a volunteer role as an aide in a high school classroom was not actually the case. The principal planned for him to teach an English Literature class for 45 freshmen in high school (ages ranging from 14-15). A big difference in responsibility. As you can imagine, he was a bit intimidated by what was expected. Along with his teaching responsibility, he would also assist coaching the track and swim teams.

At this point, you may be wondering how education is structured in Swaziland. Is is similar to that in the US or different?

Mackenzie's class

Students are "learners"

Education in Swaziland begins with preschool for infants and goes all the way through university. Learners (yes, that is what Swazis call students) spend their first seven years in primary school, grades 1-7, ending with a compulsory exam. From there, learners move to junior secondary high school for three years where they complete general education classes culminating in a public exam. Once they pass this exam and earn their junior certificate, learners can progress to senior secondary high school, which is two years of study. At the end of senior secondary level, learners sit for a national exam and those who pass earn their Swaziland General Certificate of Secondary Education (similar to our high school diploma) and International General Certificate of Secondary Education (IGCSE) which is accredited by the Cambridge International Examination (CIE). Some schools offer advanced studies and all schools are encouraged to offer a minimum of six subjects.[74]

St. Mark's High School, where Mackenzie volunteered, was originally founded in 1910 by the Anglican Mission Church as a school for European pupils (whites only). In 1956, the school transitioned to the Swaziland Government Education Department. Since then, the school has become a multiracial, co-educational institution with a learner population predominately Swazi and few other races and nationalities. St. Mark's offers learners a boarding option (called hostels) and can accommodate up to 200 individuals (male and female) who want to live on campus. St. Mark's curriculum follows the Cambridge International Advanced Level Syllabus which is one of the most recognized university entry qualifications worldwide. Exams are conducted using the UK model.

Fortunately, one of Mackenzie's greatest strengths is his adaptability.

When he learned that he would be teaching a class, Mackenzie sought help from others including Peter. The principal and the other teachers were extremely supportive. Throughout the term, he was mentored by the Head of the English Department, Mrs. Dlamini, whose class he was teaching for the term. She was teaching another class with the same material so they wrote lesson plans together. She worked with Mackenzie to make sure everything was going smoothly and that the students were learning the same material as their peers in other classes.

As a result, Mackenzie's confidence in his ability to teach students grew over time. He also became much more comfortable with public speaking. Prior to this, he had always disliked speaking in front of both small and large groups of people. By the end of his three months, he had acquired the ability to speak confidently in front of the entire school assembly.

Surprisingly, Mackenzie even tapped me to help. The principal had asked all the teachers to integrate a career planning component in their classes. It was gratifying when he contacted me about coming up with an activity that he could use. I found a couple of excellent activities that he successfully used with his students to introduce strengths—something he was familiar with.

Other things that Mackenzie adapted to included the country's drought. When he arrived in Swaziland, it was summer, and the country was suffering from a severe drought. This was unusual for Swaziland. Water was shut off and rationed several times. The government arranged for water to be delivered by truck and tanks were filled for use at schools and other essential businesses.

When learning about Mackenzie's background in playing different sports, Principal Zwane was very excited. She was eager for him to teach swimming lessons at the school and coach the track team. Mackenzie sent us a photo of the pool located on school grounds and expressed some concern about the water quality and safety for swimmers. When I saw the photo, I thought it looked like a science experiment!

Eventually, the pool was cleaned and Mackenzie was ready to begin swim lessons, though, he had a rough start! At the first swim practice, Mackenzie arrived and found a large group of students who had signed up. He had not expected this. He was also expecting to have another teacher helping, but the teacher had left school that afternoon and had not returned.

St. Marks pool - ready for swim practice

This left Mackenzie to run the first practice. When he asked how many knew how to swim, a number of the students raised their hands. When he asked how many had a swimsuit to wear, he got the same response. Mackenzie then went into change into his suit as he had come directly from the classroom.

What happened next could have been something out of a movie. When Mackenzie came out of the changing room, all the students were in the pool, most with their clothes on, happily splashing and horsing around. In relating the story to Mike and me during one of our calls a week later, he said all he could think about was the news headline: "Volunteer Teacher Responsible for Drowning at St. Mark's!"

His initial response was one of fear for the students. He yelled at them to get out of the pool with as much authority as he could muster. However, after taking a second to pause and think about what was best, he adjusted his tone and approach. Mackenzie was able to laugh about the situation later on, but, in the moment, he was tested to handle something that he was not prepared for.

Embracing opportunities

Outside of school, Mackenzie found that he had a lot of free time, so he took the opportunity to read for fun (remember that was one of the reasons he wanted to take time off from school). Peter and Precious lived across from the US Embassy and Mackenzie had access to its library. Over the three months he read over 30 books. One was a very influential text, *The challenge for Africa: A new vision* written by Wangari Maathai, a Kenyan social and environmental activist and winner of the Nobel Peace Prize.[75] The book significantly impacted Mackenzie's thinking throughout his time in Swaziland, as well as back in the US, in regard to social and environmental issues.

Living in Africa, Mackenzie was able to comprehend what the author argued—that Africa needed to solve its own problems through grass-roots, community organizing. International organizations, though well-intentioned, often caused more challenges and their support was not sustainable.

He was also asked to play on the US Embassy soccer team. One of the players was from San Diego—where Mackenzie had spent time visiting my oldest brother Jeff and sister-in-law Agnes. It made him feel connected. He took long runs in the country and enjoyed seeing the geography of the area; it reminded him of southern California and the scenery around Los Angeles. He also found that his pace of life was much slower than in the US.

When Mike and I would check in with Mackenzie by phone using WhatsApp, we found ourselves enjoying rich conversations with him that would last quite awhile. I got the sense, at times, that he was a bit homesick. I also could see that he was learning a great deal from this experience. Some of the stereotypes and myths about South Africa were highlighted during this time. As I previously shared, Mackenzie lived with one of the more affluent families in Mbabane so his experience was not one of hardship and poverty.

He also experienced what it was like to be a minority. He was white living in an almost all-black community. Even to this day, the experience of being a minority provides a context for him as he engages in racial and social justice causes.

Six degrees of separation

Mackenzie said that when he walked around Mbabane that he was often mistaken for a student of Waterford School. When he asked Peter about Waterford, Peter told him that Waterford had been established in the 1960s as a result of apartheid. Waterford was private and the first multi-racial school in South Africa, whereas St. Mark's was public and primarily served blacks.[76] Peter shared that two of Nelson Mandela's children had attended Waterford. Curious, Mackenzie decided to visit the school and learn more about it.

What happened next was a lesson in the six degrees of separation.[77]

Mackenzie arrived at Waterford one afternoon and spoke to a couple of employees at the school. During the conversation, another employee walked by, overheard the conversation, and stopped to talk to Mackenzie. He shared that he was an alum of Waterford School and had recently returned to work at the school after completing his college degree in the US.

And where do you think this individual graduated from?

Colorado College—the school in Colorado Springs where I had worked for 8½ years and where Mackenzie had spent time enrolled in daycare! At one time he'd even considered applying to CC.

As the two chatted about their connection to CC, they learned that they also had a mutual acquaintance, Megan Nicklaus. Mackenzie knew Megan because she had worked with me at Vanderbilt before leaving to become the Director of the CC Career Center. The CC alum had worked with Megan when he was a student needing career guidance.

The alum was familiar with Woodland Park—the small town where we had lived prior to our move to Nashville—as his host family lived there. And even more interesting, he was applying to the Vanderbilt's Higher Education masters program housed at Peabody College, which was located only two blocks from our townhome in Nashville.

When I was at Vanderbilt, part of our efforts to build core competencies included introducing students to the principles behind the six degrees of separation. We felt it was important to help them understand how to tap into an underlying network of individuals through existing relationships. We would utilize a simulation to illustrate the six degrees of separation for students.

Mackenzie's experience was so much richer for meeting the CC alum at the Waterford School, because it afforded him a real-life example of the six degrees of separation. He was able to understand how connected the world has become.

Mackenzie's experience in Swaziland is difficult to summarize in just a chapter. An entire book could be written about the lessons he learned during his three months living there. In reality, it is Mackenzie's story to share. I can only reflect on his experience from the perspective of a parent and one who has worked with emerging adults for many years.

Class field trip

Continuing the "learning journey"

Mackenzie's time in Swaziland was the bookend to his "gap year." I would rather describe it as part of a learning journey, one in which he would find himself again and grow in ways that a classroom environment would not have necessarily nurtured. His journey had begun in NOLS in August, and Swaziland was just a continuation of this journey.

At the same time that Mackenzie was on his learning journey, I had been on one of my own. I had left Vanderbilt in December and was in the process of trying to figure out what might be next for me professionally. It was during this time that the idea of this book began.

One day, in late March, I received the following email from Mackenzie. I share it with you to illustrate the type of impact alternative learning experiences can have on your child.

Dear Funk & Myers,

Firstly, I just downloaded the app called Whatspp. It's really popular here in Swaziland, and should be an easy and cheap way for me to message you guys in the US. So if you all want to get the app, that would be sweet!

On another note, this is the quote (more of an essay really) on the trapeze swings that I was telling you guys about on the phone a couple weeks ago. While it is a tad repetitive at times, the core meaning is wonderful and has many interesting points. It's not short, so make sure to take a little time to read it.

****

The Parable of the Trapeze

Turning the Fear of Transformation into the Transformation of Fear by Danaan Parry[78]

Sometimes I feel that my life is a series of trapeze swings. I'm either hanging on to a trapeze bar swinging along or, for a few moments in my life, I'm hurtling across space in between trapeze bars.

Most of the time, I spend my life hanging on for dear life to my trapeze bar-of-the-moment. It carries me along a certain steady rate of swing and I have the feeling that I'm in control of my life. I know most of the right questions and even some of the right answers. But once in a while, as I'm merrily (or not so merrily) swinging along, I look ahead of me into the distance, and what do I see? I see another trapeze bar swinging toward me. It's empty, and I know, in that place in me that knows, that this new trapeze bar has my name on it. It is my next step, my growth, my aliveness going to get me. In my heart-of-hearts I know that, for me to grow, I must release my grip on the present, well-known bar to move to the new one.

Each time it happens to me, I hope (no, I pray) that I won't have to grab the new one. But in my knowing place I know that I must totally release my grasp on my old bar, and for some moment in time, I must hurtle across space before I can grab onto the new bar. Each time I am filled with terror. It doesn't matter that in all my previous hurtles across the void of unknowing, I have always made it. Each time I am afraid that I will miss, that I will be crushed in unseen rock in the bottomless chasm between the bars. But I do it anyway. Perhaps this is the essence of what the Mystics call the faith experience. No guarantees, no net, no insurance policy, but you do it anyway because somehow, to keep hanging onto that old bar is no longer on the list of alternatives. And so, for an eternity that can last a microsecond or a thousand lifetimes, I soar across the dark void of the past that is gone, the future that is not yet here.

It's called transition. I have come to believe that it is the only place that real change occurs. I mean REAL change, not the pseudo-change that only lasts until the next time my old buttons get punched.

I have noticed that, in our culture, this transition zone is looked upon as a "no-thing," a place no-place between places. Sure, the old trapeze bar was real, and that new one coming towards me, I hope that's real too. But the void between? That's just a scary, confusing, disorienting "nowhere" that must be gotten through as fast and as unconsciously as possible. What a waste!

I have a sneaking suspicion that the transition zone is the only real thing, and the bars are illusions we dream up to avoid the void, where the real change, the real growth occurs for us. Whether or not my hunch is true, it remains that the transition zones in our lives are incredibly rich places. They should be honored, even favored. Yes, with all the pain and fear and feelings of being out-of-control that can (but not necessarily) accompany transitions, they are still the most alive, most growth-filled, passionate, expansive moments in our lives.

And so transformation of fear may have nothing to do with making fear go away, but rather with giving ourselves permission to "hang out" in the transition between trapeze bars. Transforming our need to grab that new bar, any bar, is allowing ourselves to dwell in the only place where change really happens. It can be terrifying. It can also be enlightening, in the true sense of the word. Hurtling through the void, we just may learn how to fly.

****

We have definitely had our share of "weightless" leaps of faith from one trapeze bar to another as a family. Not a lot of parents stop work, pull their kids out of school, and decide to go trek around Australia for three months. This was an area between the trapeze swings, a transitional period, an area of growth for us as a family. Even though Stu and I were young, I'm sure we could all say as a family that the Australia Walkabout was and still is a defining moment for each of us, and had far reaching consequences and influences into the rest of our lives.

Mom, I hope you read this and take to heart that it's ok to not be holding onto a trapeze swing. It's OK to float for a while, to live "differently," to not worry about grabbing onto another trapeze swing just yet and enjoy the weightlessness of the in-between stage.

Dad, as you said on the phone, you are going to be faced in the near or not so near future with the challenge of deciding whether or not to let go of the trapeze swing you're on and leap for another.

Stu: I know you will take to heart the words of this essay, whether they come to mean something tomorrow or years down the road, only time will tell. I know in the future you will have many leaps of faith between swings, just as I am having one right now. Your desire to already plan on taking a gap year shows that you are unafraid of the next trapeze swing, and of the transitional period in-between.

When I think back to how close I was to not taking a gap year, it's scary. I'm sure mom and dad will remember, but I was sold on going to college. Two weeks in a row of visiting Tulane and then Miami had me in a college frenzy. I couldn't get enough. Parties, sports, girls, beaches, new cities to explore. The possibilities were endless.

Anything seemed better than the pointless, mundane life of high school. I wanted to quickly jump to the next trapeze swing, not even worrying about the void in between.

However, mom, with her mystical prophetic abilities, knew a gap year would be extremely transformative for me. And it has been. The area between trapeze swings for me since setting out for NOLS on August 18th has been a crazy time of growth and change, as I'm sure you guys have caught on.

So much has happened, and now as I still hurdle through the infinite chasm, trying not to look down, the trapeze on the other side swinging towards me is not the same as it was last year.

I am still in mid-flight, still growing.

I have spent time since coming to Swaziland thinking about what life would have been like if I had gone to Miami. But I need to tell myself not to think about this, because there is no way to predict what that path would have held for me. All I know is that I am in an exceedingly strange and important transitional period in my life, and just want to thank each of you and appreciate you guys as a family for supporting my "walkabout," "my leap of faith," "my gap year and now second gap year."

I do not know what the future holds, but what I do know is that I am happy to have you three be my accompanying performers on the trapeze swings in this circus we call "Life."

Love,
Mackenzie

Mackenzie's Gap Year Plan

August – November
- Fly to Seattle. Shuttle to NOLS Base Camp – Mt Vernon, WA.
- Complete NOLS 80-day Pacific Northwest Semester.
- Shuttle to Seattle airport.

November – January
- Fly to Denver. Shuttle (Mom & Dad) to Aunt's Condo in Silverthorne.
- Get a job at ski resort in Summit County.
- Live at aunt's condo, work, & ski.
- Re-visit College Decision.
- Return to Nashville. Prepare for 3 mos. Swaziland.
  + Explore 2nd Gap Year – Hike AT

January – April
- Fly to Johannesburg, South Africa. Meet host family & travel by car to Mbabane, Swaziland.
- Volunteer at St. Mark's High School for one term.
- Live with Inampusa family.
- Fly from Mbabane home to Nashville.

May – ~~August~~ June
- Get a job in Nashville. Work/save $ for college/AT Hike
- ~~Begin University of Miami~~. Hike AT instead
- Take 2nd Gap Year. New Plan.

Mackenzie's 2nd Gap Year Plan

May - June
- WORK + save $ for AT hike
- Prepare for hike

June
- Drive to Harpers Ferry with Mom, Dad, + Stuart
- Begin AT northbound hike with Mom, Dad, + Stuart

July - September
- Continue solo hike northbound. Re-supply/3days
- Summit Mt. Katahdin - AT northern terminus
- Return to Harpers Ferry

September - December
- Begin southbound solo hike at Harpers Ferry
- Complete thru hike of AT - Springer Mtn, GA
- Return to Nazzy

December - January
- Apply to colleges
- Find job in Nazzy. Save $ for college.

~~April~~ February - August
- WORK
- Make college decision
- Begin college

What You Can Do

1. Consider the reaction that your parent or parents might have had if you informed them of your plan to go to another country by yourself. Would you respond the same way or handle it differently?
2. Discuss with your young adult the value of understanding connections and give non-work examples from your life.
3. Share with your young adult the concept of flexible planning and give an example when you had to change plans.

Notes

St. Marks teaching team

On a field trip

Fun with Gabriel

Selfie with Laston

Am I Too Late?

Chapter 10
Trail Magic on the AT

The journey of a thousand miles begins with a single step.
—Lao Tzu, Chinese philosopher and founder of Taoism

First, let me start by sharing a little bit about the Appalachian Trail, usually shortened to simply the AT. Before Mackenzie's decision to hike the AT, I knew little about the trail, so sharing details with those of you who might not be familiar with the AT will provide a context for what Mackenzie was attempting to do.

The AT is one of the world's top ten longest hiking trails that stretches 2,193 miles between Georgia and Maine, crossing 14 states. The trail is managed by the National Park Service, US Forest Service, and the non-profit Appalachian Trail Conservancy.[79] Since 2010, the number of thru-hikers attempting to complete the AT each year has grown to approximately 3,700, but only 25% finish their hike. Individuals can hike northbound, starting in Georgia and ending in Maine, southbound, which begins in Maine and ends in Georgia, or do a flip flop thru-hike, starting somewhere in the middle of the AT, completing one-half, returning to the middle and completing the other half.[80] When a hiker completes a thru-hike, they are considered a 2,000 miler and are recognized by the Appalachian Trail Conservancy.

The decision to hike the Appalachian Trail

When Mackenzie returned from his three months in Swaziland, he began to question his decision to hike the AT. A number of his friends had returned home to Nashville after finishing their first year of college and he was having fun catching up with them.

One afternoon, after being home for three weeks, Mackenzie said to me, "I don't know, Mom. I am not so sure that I should hike the AT this fall. A lot of my friends are telling me that it would be a mistake and that I should go ahead and start at Miami."

Mackenzie's dilemma is one many students face sometime during their gap year. Gap year research data reveals that many "gappers" choose to enroll in the college from which they originally deferred enrollment. Others choose to apply to a different college mid-way through their gap year because they have decided their deferred college is not where they want to go. A few decide to take a second year before starting college.

"Why don't you go talk to Mr. Flatau? He might be able to help you think about your options," I suggested.

George Flatau had been one of Mackenzie's favorite teachers at USN. He had been a mentor, advisor, and a positive and motivating influence for him as his cross-country coach. Mackenzie looked up to him and respected his opinion.

"Great idea. I think I will walk over now and see if he is around," Mackenzie replied.

At this point, we lived in a townhome on Music Row, two blocks from Vanderbilt and USN. It was convenient being so close to school and work. USN would be finishing its academic year so Mackenzie knew that George would most likely be around, as well as other teachers he might want to check in with.

A few hours later, Mackenzie returned home. He appeared much more relaxed.

"So how did it go? Were you able to talk to Flatau?" I asked.

"It was great talking to him, Mom," Mackenzie replied. "I also got to talk to Espy (he had been Mackenzie's French teacher) and they both said that college could wait. Hiking the AT would be something that I would never regret."

I was relieved that he was feeling more comfortable about his decision to delay starting college and take a "second gap year."

What would a second year of discovery look like?

In December, mid-way through his first gap year, Mackenzie had articulated a serious desire to thru-hike the Appalachian Trail beginning the following summer. It would take him approximately five to six months to complete so that meant he would forego college another year.

When he returned home from Swaziland in late April, it was clear that he still had a "calling" to thru-hike the AT. He had continued to research what it would take to complete the hike while he was abroad, and remained committed to making the hike. His plan was to begin in late June and finish in early December.

After that, he would return home, and apply to colleges in December and January for a Fall 2017 start. He also planned to get a job in January and work through the spring and summer before starting college.

The art of flexible planning

At least that was the plan. It was a "flexible" plan and very different from his first year plan, which structured his time in specific ways. It is the type of plan that I help individuals develop when coaching them. Creating a flexible plan allows individuals to adapt and adjust to changing circumstances and remain open to new ideas and opportunities that present themselves.

Which is what happened for Mackenzie.

But I am getting ahead of myself.

After Mackenzie's conversation with his teachers at USN about hiking the AT, he committed fully to the plan. Because of the time constraints of reaching the northern terminus of the trail, Mt. Katahdin in Maine, before it closed for the winter, Mackenzie decided that he would use a flip flop thru-hike approach. He would begin hiking north from Harpers Ferry, West Virginia, in late June with the goal of summiting Katahdin in September and then return to Harpers Ferry and hike south to the other AT terminus at Springer Mountain in Georgia.

Mike, Stuart, and I planned to hike the first two weeks with Mackenzie; we thought it would be great fun as a family to start this adventure with him. We would all drive to Harpers Ferry, hike together, and at the end of two weeks Mackenzie would continue on. The rest of us would catch a shuttle or some mode of transport back to our car in Harpers Ferry and return to Nashville.

While he prepared for the hike, Mackenzie worked at a local arborist company, lifeguarded at the Vandy Rec Center, and for a week at the end of May, he helped move Vandy students out of their off-campus apartments. This allowed him to collect items Vandy students left behind at the end of the spring semester. He sold the items at a two-day garage sale in June and raised $1,000 for his hike. It was amazing to see how much "stuff" was left behind that Mackenzie was able to collect and sell. Of course, Mike and I were roped into the enterprise by letting him store all the items in our garage, patio area, and townhome for a short while (sheer chaos!) and of course helping with the garage sale. Items that did not sell were taken to Goodwill. If Mackenzie had not taken on this project, most of these items would have ended up in the trash.

Unfortunately, our plans to hike with Mackenzie did not come to fruition. At the same time he was preparing for the AT, Mike and I were in the process of making a decision about our future. I had received an offer for employment that would keep us in Nashville and Mike had received a couple of employment offers—one in Oregon and the other in Indonesia.

With my separation from Vanderbilt in December of 2015, Mike had felt free to pursue faculty positions across the US and internationally. He had finished his PhD from Vanderbilt in 2012 and had managed to secure work at the university, but it was not his desired faculty appointment.

The move to Portland

After deliberating as a family (using our famous decision matrix), we decided to move to Portland, Oregon. Mike accepted the offer for a tenure-track faculty appointment at the Oregon Institute of Technology - Portland Metro campus, and agreed to begin first of August. One of his responsibilities was to stand up a new research and development advanced manufacturing facility north of Portland.

Once the decision was made, we made a quick trip to Portland and were lucky to secure a furnished apartment and arrange for Stuart's enrollment in high school for the fall. Returning to Nashville, we spent the remaining part of June preparing for our cross-country move planned for July 6th. This meant scrapping our plans to hike the AT with Mackenzie.

At the end of June, Mike and Stuart drove Mackenzie to Harpers Ferry, staying one-night in Johnson City with my niece Kelsi to break up the trip. I had drawn the lucky straw to stay behind to continue the work of downsizing. Lucky? Right!

Beginning the trail at Harpers Ferry

The hike begins!

The trio arrived in Harpers Ferry and located the trailhead, which is marked by the AT iconic symbol—the White Blaze. After snapping the requisite photo showing Mackenzie striking out on his thru-hike, Mike and Stuart saw him off by hiking a couple of miles, and then turned back so they could return to Nashville. We were planning to move the following week.

I was a little sad not to have hiked the AT—maybe someday. Of course, there is always the Pacific Crest Trail not too far from where I am now!

Late June of 2016 found Mackenzie beginning his next learning journey. Soon thereafter, Mike, Stuart, and I began our new chapter in Portland. Over the next several months, as I was settling into a new home and city, I would periodically send Mackenzie packages that he requested. As the weather changed, he needed different clothing and other items that he could not purchase easily in towns where he re-supplied. He had left a plastic tub labeled "Mackenzie's AT" so when he needed something, I would retrieve it from the bin and send it along. For Mackenzie to receive a package, I had to address it to him in care of one of the post offices that was near the AT, and they would hold the package for him until he could pick it up. It was amazingly simple.

Periodically, he would check in with us. I was surprised how often he had cell coverage on the AT. I thought it would be more like his NOLS or Swaziland experiences when it had been difficult at times to connect due to limited Internet access and phone service. But that was not the case on the AT, so we had the opportunity to hear how he was doing along the way.

SOS Sunshine and "trail angels"

Before Mackenzie began his hike, I wondered how he would handle the loneliness of hiking solo for five to six months. Would he find it too isolating since he was naturally a social person? However, I did not need to be concerned.

Throughout the summer and fall, Mackenzie experienced the community that is a large part of the AT. He met many "trail angels" who provided hospitality and support all along the trail to hikers. From meals to rides to offers of housing, he grew to appreciate the trail magic.

He also enjoyed spending time with friends who periodically joined him to hike a short section of the AT. One friend, Skye Cameron, joined him for four weeks that coincided with Mackenzie's 19th birthday in early August. As luck would have it, they were hiking the section of the AT in western Massachusetts located about seven miles from my sister and brother-in-law's summer cabin, lovingly nicknamed Camp Machu Picchu.

Melodie, my saint of a sister, and her husband Steve, picked up Mackenzie and Skye from one of the access points to the trail and transported them to the cabin for some TLC—hot showers, beds, and lots of good, nourishing food. I say "saint" because AT thru-hikers are known for their rather pungent body odor when you get near them. Understandable, since few take time to shower and launder the clothing they wear hiking.

Sunshine and Skye

After enjoying my sister and brother-in-law's hospitality at Camp Machu Picchu, Mackenzie and Skye were dropped off at the trail to continue hiking north. When his four weeks were up, Skye left Mackenzie to start his second year at Bates College in Maine. He would rejoin Mackenzie for the final climb to Mt. Katahdin in September.

Mackenzie continued north, staying at designated AT shelters along the way and re-supplying every third or fourth day. He had chosen to use one of the ultra-light backpacks and worked to maintain no more than 30 pounds of weight to carry. However, it was important for him to pack enough food to maintain the energy needed to hike 20-25 miles/day. Mackenzie strived to eat a goal of 3,000 calories/day to meet the demands of the long-distance hike. He found that resupplying was fairly easy due to the small towns near the trail that were part of the AT community who welcomed AT thru-hikers.

Following the traditions of thru-hikers, Mackenzie adopted a trail name —Sunshine. It was a name he had been given on his NOLS course. Later on, Mackenzie was given an addition to his name: SOS Sunshine.

One evening, Mackenzie arrived at a designated campsite and shelter and left his backpack to more freely hike down to a water source. Before leaving to find water, he talked to two fellow hikers at the campsite who had become friends. This happened a lot on the AT as he would find himself running into the same hikers and end up hiking with them for a period of time.

While trying to locate water, it grew dark and Mackenzie lost his way. He did not have his headlamp and could not see where he was going because of the foliage and the forest that surrounded him. His phone battery had died and his backup charger was with his backpack. He told me, months later, that it was the only time that he ever felt truly scared.

Trying not to panic, he decided to stop where he was and think about what his options were—including spending the night until daylight when he could better navigate. He also began calling loudly for his two friends, shouting their names into the night. Luckily, the two hikers heard him and were able to locate him in the dark and assisted him with getting back to the campsite. Hence, the name SOS Sunshine.

Lost on trail

Getting lost on the Appalachian Trail is not uncommon. One step off the trail where the brush is thick and there are no markers can result in disorientation.

Being "lost on trail" reminds me of the many college students I've worked with who were confused about their direction in life and looking for trail markers—signs that pointed them in the right direction. I knew students who graduated and had still not found the signs.

Fortunately, Mackenzie did not panic when he found himself lost. A woman hiking the AT in the same area two years before had gotten lost and had fallen to her death.[81] Her body was found a year later. He was very lucky, indeed!

As planned, Mackenzie made it to Maine in mid-September and summited Mt. Katahdin, completing the first part of his flip flop thru-hike. After a two-week break, he returned to Harpers Ferry and began hiking southbound toward Georgia.

Northern terminus - Mt. Katahdin

It was the southbound hike where Mackenzie would face some significant challenges. One of the first days back on trail, he suffered a hip injury, making it painful to hike. He shared this news with Mike and me on one of our check-in calls. We happened to have a good friend Carol (who had known Mackenzie since he was a baby) visiting us at the time and, when she learned of his injury, she called a friend of hers who lived in Virginia, and asked for help. Not even knowing my son, this friend of a friend drove an hour to pick up Mackenzie, took care of him for three days, and returned him back to the trail. Amazing. The kindness of so many people who helped Mackenzie along the way was truly humbling.

The three-day break was just what he needed. Though his hip still bothered him, Mackenzie was able to return to hiking a good number of miles per day. If he was to complete his thru-hike, he had to keep up an average of 20-25 miles/day.

Appalachian Trail Conservancy HQ
The sign on this building in Harpers Ferry, WV represents the psychological half-way point of the 2,189-mile Appalachian Trail. Hikers walking the entire A.T. are photographed here.
www.appalachiantrail.org

Harpers Ferry, Round 2!
Hope you guys are well.
Ready to hit the trail
and finish what I started.
Springer Mountain here I come!
- SoS Sunshine (Mackenzie)

Funk+Myers Family
1209 SW 6th Ave #701
Portland, OR 97204

Decision time: fires in the Great Smokies

Due to a particularly dry summer, as Mackenzie hiked south, he ran into fires that had begun in North Carolina and spread to the Great Smoky Mountains. At times he was not sure he could get through certain sections of the trail, as some areas were being closed to hikers for safety reasons. A big decision moment came when he had only 300 miles left to hike, and a section of the trail closed because of the fires.

One morning in late November, I received a call from Mackenzie. I was surprised to hear from him, because we usually coordinated a time to speak in the evening. He shared with me that he had just heard that a hundred mile section of the trail was closed due to fires. He wasn't sure what to do. I could just hear in his voice the disappointment and almost resignation that he would not be able to finish. So I did what I do best—I brainstormed options with him.

Potentially, he could catch a ride to where the trail was open (yes—hitchhiking is the norm for hiking the AT), skip the closed section, and continue hiking south until the trail reopened. He would then hitchhike back to where he had left the trail and complete the section that had been closed. Or, maybe he would just stop hiking, get my niece Kelsi (who lived an hour away) to pick him up and take him to the closest airport, where he would fly home to Portland. He would then return in the spring and finish the hike.

> **On November 28, 2016, a raging inferno swept through the Great Smoky Mountains National Park and into the city of Gatlinburg, Tennessee killing 14 people and injuring 190 more. Damage caused by the fires was estimated at over $500 million. 2,460 structures were damaged or destroyed.**

Mackenzie was so close, and I knew it would be hard for him to return once he left the AT. The other option he came up with was to stay put for 3-4 days and see if the fires cleared and the trail reopened. Ultimately, he decided the latter was his best option. His luck held, the trail reopened, and he was able to continue on south toward Georgia.

By then, it was early December and Mackenzie was pushing up against his deadline to finish in December. Weather had changed, making it difficult to hike safely. With temperatures dropping below freezing at night and snowfall, Mackenzie knew he needed to finish soon. The trail was becoming too treacherous to hike

He set his goal to summit Springer Mountain, the southern terminus in Georgia, at sunset on December 17th. He had arranged for a friend from his NOLS course, who lived near Atlanta, to meet him. She would put him up for the night and then drive him to the Atlanta airport, where he would catch a flight to Portland. As you may recall, we'd completed our move there during Mackenzie's hike of the AT. Due to the delays caused by the fires, I had already rescheduled his flight a couple of times (gotta love Southwest!)

Anxious to see if he would meet his goal, Mike and I began to check our phones at night to see what progress he had made that day (GPS

169

capability of iPhones made this possible). We were able to track Mackenzie's movement and saw when he stopped at a shelter for the night or when he kept on hiking to the next shelter.

Did he make it?

Yes!

During his last 35 miles, Mackenzie ended up running into the night using his headlamp to see.

Thru-hike complete!

Like Swaziland, the AT thru-hike will be forever a defining life experience and accomplishment for Mackenzie. He met many hikers during his five and a half months on the trail, from veterans "walking off the war" to weary professionals seeking to connect with a purpose that was missing in their lives.

In 2016, the year that Mackenzie hiked the AT, only 20% who started their thru-hike finished. He was one of the roughly 685 individuals who completed a solo thru-hike that year.

From other hikers, Mackenzie heard about a documentary that REI was filming about the AT, called *Paul's Boots,* and encouraged us to check it out.[82] We did and were inspired and uplifted by Paul's story. The film provides a moving account of hikers accepting the call of a widow whose husband had always wanted to hike the AT but died before he could.

To fulfill his dream, AT hikers volunteer to carry his heavy size 13 boots from Georgia to Maine, adding extra weight to their packs. Throughout the film, different hikers carry Paul's boots and share their stories. The reasons they have chosen to thru-hike the AT vary, but it is clear from their stories that the hike has profoundly changed them. Mackenzie had the good fortune to meet one of the hikers carrying Paul's boots, so he personally connected with the film.

I encourage you to watch the film with your college-bound child as it highlights what can happen when an individual chooses to embrace the challenge of taking a different path, especially one that entails breaking away from what is expected to engage in an alternative experience to learn and discover.

Mackenzie's journey not only involved hiking the 2,100 miles of the AT. As he walked, he listened to books and podcasts downloaded to his phone on topics that included philosophy, ethics, history, and more. As the miles went by, he walked, experienced, and learned.

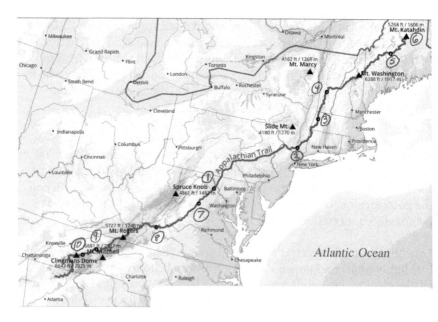

1 - Harpers Ferry
2 - Skye joins
3 - Mel & Steve - Machu Picchu
4 - Skye leaves
5 - Lost on trail
6 - Skye joins for Katahdin
7 - Hip injury
8 - Four Pines Hostel - good friends!
9 - Kelsi & Josh
10 - Hiker Thanksgiving

Key moments on the trail

Champion of Useless Endeavors
An essay by Mackenzie

The brisk winter breeze rushed through my hair as the faint glow of the quickly fading sun filtered through the bare branches. I was worn out and exhausted from hiking 109 miles over the past three days, but just ahead I saw the once distant sign, "Springer Mountain-Southern Terminus of the Appalachian Trail: 1 Mile." It was the final mile of a 2,189 mile journey.

I began to run. Roots, branches, rocks, and icy sheets flashed past my sight, but I paid them no attention. My mind flitted to memories of the long walk, from climbing mountains and pushing through pains to forging friendships and learning life lessons. Up and up I ran as the sun slipped down and down. At last, I ran out into an open clearing, and saw the bronze plaque I had been walking towards for thousands of miles. I kissed the words that marked the end to my journey, and knelt before the plaque. No tears flowed from my eyes. No existential epiphany filled my mind. Instead, an overwhelming sense of relief and accomplishment washed over my entire body. I turned away from the plaque and looked out over southern Georgia basking in a vivid red sunset, and thought to myself "I did it."

The journey had taken me on foot through 14 states from Maine to Georgia along the Appalachian Mountain Range, ascending and descending in elevation the equivalent to climbing Mount Everest 16 times.

As I stood beside the plaque, I realized it was almost a year to the day from when I sat down with my parents on a cold December evening in 2015, explaining to them that I wanted to take another gap year, another year after high school before furthering my formal education. I had just completed an incredibly transformative 80 day semester at the National Outdoor Leadership School and in January, I was headed to Swaziland to teach high school English and coach swimming and track and field. However, I kept finding myself drawn to the idea of hiking the entire Appalachian Trail (AT). I spent numerous hours researching the footpath stretching along the east coast, reading stories, and looking at gear reviews. I weighed the pros and cons of taking another year before going to college and decided to follow my dream. I worked to save up enough money to fund the journey and in June, with the support of my family and friends, I set off on the trail in the heat of summer.

I finished hiking the trail in December, completing a seemingly impossible dream of mine. The experience of hiking the AT is something I cherish as a pivotal time of self-exploration, maturation, and personal freedom. While walking in the woods for months on end does not directly solve the myriad problems our world faces today, the lessons I learned shape my perspectives and inform my actions in "the front country."

I realize that the moments of self-discovery that take place during seemingly useless endeavors like a thru-hike of the AT, are what I take back to society and use to initiate some positive change in the world.

The AT taught me the invaluable lessons of persistence and hard work, of camaraderie, and of appreciating the simple things in life. Amidst tumultuous and frightening world events, my faith in humanity was continually renewed by the kindness I received from absolute strangers. Most of all, the trail taught me that no matter how grandiose and daunting your goal may be, every step you take is progress towards accomplishing your dreams. No dream is too big, nor any mountain too high. All you have to do is start climbing, and the rest will follow.

Mackenzie's 2nd Gap Year Plan

May -June
- Work + save $ for AT hike
- Prepare for hike
- + Family decision- move to PDX. Trip to PDX.

June
- Drive to Harpers Ferry with ~~Mom~~, Dad, + Stuart
- Begin AT northbound solo hike ~~with Mom, Dad, + Stuart~~

July -September
- Continue solo hike northbound. Resupply/ 3days
- Summit Mt. Katahdin - AT northern terminus
- Return to Harpers Ferry
- + 2 week Break -Visit friends Boston + Tampa

~~September~~ October - December
- Begin southbound solo hike at Harpers Ferry
- Complete thru hike of AT - Springer Mtn, GA
- ~~Return to Nozzy~~ Travel to PDX

December - January
- Apply to colleges
- Find job in Nozzy. Save $ for college.

~~April~~ February -August
- WORK
- Make college decision
- Begin college

What You Can Do

1. Ask your young adult as they engage in the different activities during their time away, "What life skills can be gleaned from these experiences?"
2. Reflecting on your life or your young adult's life, were there times that you found yourself "lost on trail?" What did you do?
3. Challenge your young adult to engage in activities that encourages problem-solving and tests their endurance.

Notes

Trail Magic on the AT

On the AT

Am I Too Late?

Chapter 11
Mystic Winds

A Ship in Harbor Is Safe, but That Is Not What Ships Are Built For
—John A. Shedd

It goes without saying that gap years are full of twists and turns. You begin with a rough plan that will change many times as obstacles and opportunities present themselves.

After a family visit to Southern California from our new home in Portland, Mackenzie and I were heading north on the California freeway when he looked up from his laptop: "Mom, I am going to apply to this Williams-Mystic Program that Neil sent me info about."

Neil was one of Mackenzie's closest friends from high school.

Earlier in the day, we had dropped Mike and Stuart off at the John Wayne Airport in Santa Ana. My generous sister in law, who frequently traveled Southwest, had used her travel points to purchase tickets for both of them to fly home to Portland while Mackenzie and I drove. It was New Year's Day, and they needed to get back home in time to start the winter term. Mackenzie and I were returning home by car since our schedules were flexible and we could take two or three days to make the long drive from southern California to Portland. It would be fun to do a little sightseeing along the way.

"That was nice of him to think of you," I replied. "How did he hear about the program?"

"It was in the latest issue of the Williams College alumni newsletter. Neil is on the mailing list because his sister Sasha graduated from there. You remember her, don't you? She came to my high school graduation party. Anyway, Neil saw this article about the Williams-Mystic Semester Coastal

Studies Program and forwarded it to me thinking I would have an interest."

A call to sea

Mackenzie continued enthusiastically, "The program sounds really cool! You get to spend a semester studying the ocean and coastal areas of the Atlantic and the Pacific. Williams runs the program in partnership with the Mystic Seaport Museum in Mystic, Connecticut. You actually live at the seaport and take classes on maritime history, literature, science, and policy. What's even more cool is that there are three different field seminars you get to do during the semester that are hands-on. One of the field experiences you even get to live on a tall ship in the Caribbean!"

Mystic Seaport

"Sounds interesting," I replied. But I was thinking to myself "expensive" and not something we could afford. Williams College was one of the top private liberal arts colleges in the US (annual tuition costs were over $50K).

Mackenzie continued, "I know I don't qualify. It says that applicants have to be enrolled at an accredited college or university and be a junior or senior in good standing to be considered. I haven't even started college."

Not wanting to squelch his enthusiasm, but needing to be realistic, I asked, "What does it cost?"

"It says that the program costs $33K and that includes tuition, room, and board. I know that sounds really expensive, Mom, but it says that there are full and partial scholarships available. It's a long shot, but maybe they would consider me for the program. It can't hurt to email this guy named, Tom Van Winkle, the Executive Director of the program. Maybe they would be willing to waive the application requirements and allow me to apply."

After that announcement, Mackenzie quickly composed an email and sent it to the Executive Director (gotta love technology when you can email someone from the seat of a car!). In the email, he shared a bit of his background including the fact he had just completed a solo thru-hike of the AT, and expressed his interest in participating in the spring semester program.

It was at that moment, I recognized the progress Mackenzie had made in feeling more confident in his abilities. He was comfortable reaching out to a total stranger to pursue an opportunity of interest and not be worried that he would be judged in a negative light. He was open to exploring an opportunity that presented itself and had the potential for learning. Mackenzie had adopted the approach that I encourage in students and clients about flexible planning and remaining open to opportunities. Most often, these opportunities are the result of chance meetings or through connections, much like what happened in Mackenzie's case, when a friend sent him information on the Williams-Mystic opportunity.

AT transition

When thru-hikers finish the AT, there is an adjustment period as they transition back to a world with lots of stimuli. After being in nature for months, coming back to live in a town or city can be disorienting. There is a loss of the "high" that comes when your endorphins kick in as you push yourself to hike 20-30 miles a day.

Once he left the AT, Mackenzie did not have the opportunity to slowly transition back into a different and much faster-paced world.

Mackenzie's original plan was to return home after finishing the AT and spend the remainder of December and early January applying to colleges and looking for work. He had decided that the University of Miami was no longer an option and had communicated his intent to no longer enroll at the university prior to leaving for the AT.

As planned, Mackenzie made his flight from Atlanta to Portland in December but was delayed in Denver when the airport shut down because of a major snowstorm. It took a couple of days before he was able to fly out. Luckily, his aunt (the one whose condo Mackenzie stayed at in Silverthorne) was able to meet him at the airport and he spent the time with her before flying to Portland.

When he got home, everything was different. It was not our home in Nashville. We had moved to Portland while he was on the AT, so even his home was strange and unfamiliar.

After a couple of days at home (Mackenzie had barely had time to unpack), the four of us headed out by car to San Marcos in southern California to spend the holidays with family. Our original plan was to fly Southwest but, at the last minute, decided to cancel our tickets when Mackenzie was delayed getting home. We thought he would benefit from a couple of days of rest at home before traveling again and driving would allow him a little more time to get settled. The other advantage of taking a couple of days to drive was that Mackenzie would have to interact with only a few people, which would reduce the sensory overload that would have been part of flying during the holidays. We would also have the opportunity to hear about his time on the AT if he wanted to share some of his story.

We arrived in San Marcos safely and celebrated the holidays with family.

It was while we were in California that Mackenzie received the email from Neil, one of his closest friends from USN, about the Williams-Mystic Program. Neil was currently in his second year at Yale University. He had spent a lot of time with us when we lived in Nashville and we considered him part of our family. His parents, who were both from China, worked at Vanderbilt performing cancer research. They had attained their MD/PHD degrees in the US and had ended up in Nashville when Neil was young.

So what happened with Williams-Mystic?

Tom Van Winkle, the Executive Director of Williams-Mystic, decided to take a chance on Mackenzie.

Excited about Mackenzie's background and the perspective that he would bring to the spring semester cohort (usually 20 students), Tom encouraged him to submit his application, which he promptly did. This was followed by an expedited admission review process, interview, and not long after that, an offer of admissions to the program including a partial scholarship.

Mike and I were thrilled that he had been admitted to this unique program, but we were concerned about the cost. We had not budgeted for this expense and it would be a stretch on our finances. However, in our discussions with him about affordability, Mackenzie felt confident that the college would be able to provide more financial assistance. And he was right. He spoke to Tom about seeking additional funds, and to our amazement, he was offered a full-tuition scholarship to attend the spring semester program, which was scheduled to begin the last part of January.

I found out later on that Tom had a background in expeditionary learning, which was why he was so excited to have Mackenzie join the semester cohort.

Unbelievable!

Mackenzie's flexible plan to extend his gap year to hike the AT had led him to enroll in a unique semester-long program where he would learn about the three coasts of the US and the open ocean, through field experiences taught by faculty. He would also have the opportunity to explore his interests related to climate change and environmental justice —a focus of the Williams-Mystic program.

Following his original plan, Mackenzie submitted his college applications by mid-January before he embarked on his next "learning journey." A week later, on a wet and gray Saturday morning, we dropped Mackenzie off at the airport with his backpack and suitcase in hand. I found it rather surreal. Once more, we were dropping Mackenzie off at the airport as he headed toward an unknown future. But this time, instead of the Nashville airport, it was the Portland airport.

Mystic Seaport

Mackenzie flew to Boston where my sister and brother-in-law met him at the airport. They transported him to Mystic Seaport, located in Mystic, Connecticut on the Long Island Sound. He was just in time for orientation, where he met his fellow classmates, faculty, and staff of the Williams-Mystic Program. Mackenzie joined sixteen other students as part of the small cohort admitted to participate in this one-of-a kind experience. For seventeen weeks, they would study literature, history, policy, and science of oceans and coasts of the US through field experiences that offered place-based learning, and classroom instruction while they were in residence at Mystic Seaport Museum.

> "Our hope for students coming in is that they will experience an immersion into the case study we use that is the ocean and our coasts. That they will experience the complexity of the issues and they will realize over time that there are no world issues that can be solved by a single discipline. In fact, that disciplines are man-made structures that we have used to define categories of thinking, ways of thinking, out of producing knowledge. And that the world works outside of those man-made boundaries. To have an impact and to be a leader in trying to solve these issues, you must look at all these perspectives, and realize that there may be truth in all of them. That it takes a team of collaborators to solve them."
>
> Williams-Mystic Executive Director, Tom Van Winkle, Ph.D.

Students in Mackenzie's class were mostly college juniors and seniors. They came from universities and colleges from all over the US, including Yale, Harvard, University of Vermont, Stony Brook, Florida Atlantic, Bowdoin College, McDaniel College, University of Pennsylvania, St. Lawrence, University of Rhode Island, University of Puget Sound, and Williams College. Like most of his earlier years in school, Mackenzie was the youngest member of the class and had not yet started college. Would this be a problem for him, I wondered?

As part of the learning experience, students lived cooperatively in one of five houses adjacent to Mystic Seaport, one of the nation's leading maritime museums, spanning 17 coastal acres and 60 buildings. He was assigned to Johnston House along with three other classmates—two females who were vegan, and one male who, like Mackenzie, was not. Each week in residence they received $200 to cover costs of food and other necessities. They planned and prepared meals together and set up a calendar for daily and weekly chores. Pretty amazing to see what they did to ensure a functioning household! Something that took me years to learn, and that was after having two children and returning to work full-time.

What I found fascinating was that Mystic Seaport, with its museum and grounds, was the students' classroom. There were also opportunities to enjoy sailing and kayaking on the Mystic River next to the museum.

The tall ship Corwith Cramer

After getting settled in the first week, Mackenzie and the rest of his classmates flew to San Juan, Puerto Rico where they boarded the SSV Cramer, a traditionally-rigged tall ship. This would be their classroom for the next 10 days as part of the Offshore Field Seminar led by Williams-Mystic faculty and the professional crew of the SSV Corwith Cramer. Each day, faculty taught academic classes on the ship or during the occasional on-shore excursions, and the captain and crew instructed students in seamanship. Mackenzie learned how to steer, navigate, handle sails, and operate the ship around the clock.

Students were divided into three "watches" guided by a crew member and an assistant scientist. Mackenzie was part of C-watch. Each watch was assigned a six-hour shift so there was 24-hour coverage of sailing the ship. When they were on duty, they were responsible for sailing the ship and collecting water and sediment samples to be analyzed and discussed as part of the research focus of the offshore field experience. Topics of the classes ranged from law and policies governing trade and commercial fishing to geography, geology, conservation, and reef ecology.

Running an experiment

Throughout the 10 days, there was an effort to strike a balance between studies, work, and fun. During one of the on-shore excursions to St. John in the US Virgin Islands, Mackenzie and the rest of his classmates had the opportunity to swim and snorkel. Truly a special time to capture the essence of the Caribbean by exploring it through immersion.

On board the ship, students would hear the phrase 'ship, shipmate, self' several times a day. These three simple words defined a code of behavior for them to follow that was easy to understand. As one student writes in her blog post: "College education usually shies away from such direct injunctions. In this context, though, it's hard to resist. Dependent as each of us will be on the ship and its crew, taking care of those first is just good sense."[83]

She continues, "When we all ran to see the dolphins, or when we came face-to-face with the coral reefs during a snorkeling excursion, our majors became blurry, no longer the focus of our academic identity. We are learning skills that can be applied to any classroom, field of work or study, and situation. We are learning to love our wonderful world, to get re-excited about learning, and how to build a community."

"ship, shipmate, self"

The Offshore Field experience concluded with students on deck presenting their science posters and sharing data collected from three super stations: Puerto Rico trench, Puerto Rico slope, and Barracouta Bank. There was also a crew "lead" component at the end of the sailing section where one person from each watch was designated to lead. Mackenzie was voted by his fellow shipmates to lead C-watch and he really enjoyed the responsibility. It meant that he was accountable for the ship and was in charge of steering and setting direction, navigation, and directing the crew when to raise and change the sails.

They returned to shore and flew from St. Croix back to New England arriving in the middle of a blizzard. Mackenzie told us that it was quite a shock to return to frigid cold temperatures and snow after being in the Caribbean for 10 days.

Back at Mystic-Seaport, he began classes. It was easier to understand the readings *The Tempest and The Shipwreck* after having sailed on a tall ship. In addition, Mackenzie selected boat building as the maritime skill he wanted to develop. As part of the program, students were required to choose one of several maritime skills including iron work, developing sea shanties, or boat building. He also applied and secured a work-study job as a shipyard assistant helping with the restoration of the Mayflower II. The money from the job was not a lot, but it helped cover some of his incidental expenses (e.g. coffee at the local coffee shop in Mystic and ice cream at the ice cream shop). The normal cravings of a college student!

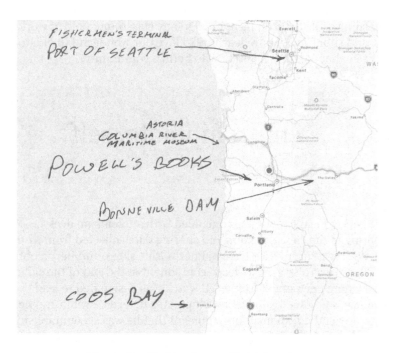

FISHERMEN'S TERMINAL
PORT OF SEATTLE

ASTORIA
COLUMBIA RIVER
MARITIME MUSEUM

POWELL'S BOOKS

BONNEVILLE DAM

COOS BAY

Mystic Pacific Northwest Field Seminar

A tugboat ride and Pike Place Market

In early March, the group flew to Seattle for their Pacific Northwest Field
Seminar. Unlike the offshore seminar, this experience included a lot of
transit time in vans. The group would start in Seattle, Washington, and
travel to southern Oregon before flying out of Portland. Mike and I were
excited about the possibility of seeing him when he was in the area.

When the group arrived in Seattle, the city became the classroom.
Mackenzie and his classmates had the opportunity to explore the city and
the port. Through on-site mini-lectures about Seattle's historical,
geological, and political dimensions, the field seminar again
demonstrated the value of place-based learning. Mackenzie learned
about the geologic identity of the region and the threats, such as
earthquakes and volcanoes that the city faced. At the Port of Seattle, he
learned about environmental initiatives and restoration projects near the
port designed to address the decades of development and industrial
pollutants impacting the port. Along with the learning there was fun

"One of the many things that makes the Williams-Mystic program so special is that it discusses the practical application of maritime issues. We all come with an academic background, but to see and understand the shipping structures that supply us with the goods and commodities we use every day is an important practical complement to our education."
—Williams-Mystic Blog

including a ride aboard a tugboat and a visit to Seattle's infamous Pike Place Market—known for its fresh fish, produce, baked goods, and crafts.

Leaving Seattle, the group traveled by van to Oregon, where a quick trip to Powell's Bookstore in Portland was a fun evening excursion. Mike, Stuart, and I met Mackenzie at Powell's for a quick catch-up. We lived just a few blocks away so the location could not have been more perfect.

Voodoo Doughnuts!

It was great seeing him and we enjoyed meeting his classmates. As a surprise, we came bearing pink boxes filled with Voodoo Doughnuts for Mackenzie to share. If you haven't heard of Voodoo Doughnuts, pay attention when you fly the next time. If you see someone carrying a pink box, you will know that they have been to Voodoo. As you can imagine, the donuts were a huge hit with Mackenzie's classmates; at least, that is what he told us.

Bonneville Dam

The next day, the group left Portland and travelled through the Columbia River Gorge to Bonneville Dam which was built in 1937 by the Army Corps of Engineers. Today, the dam illustrates the complexities of environmental and energy issues. It provides hydroelectric power to hundreds of thousands of homes, and at the same time, profoundly impacts ecosystems including salmon migration. Students were pushed to think about all facets of the issue during their dam visit and in subsequent conversations.

Next, the group traveled to Astoria where they visited the Columbia River Maritime Museum. They learned about the Columbia Bar where the Columbia River (approximately 1,200 miles long) meets the Pacific Ocean. The currents are dangerous, and many ships have been pulled under, resulting in the area being nicknamed "the graveyard of the Pacific." When Mackenzie told Mike and me about this, we were surprised. It was a fact that we did not know about Astoria, though we knew one of the Harbor Masters who navigated the ships through the pass. His children attended the same school as Stuart, and he split his time between Astoria and Portland.

That evening, Mackenzie and his classmates had fun spending the night on a decommissioned Columbia lightship docked next to the museum.

Early the next morning, they headed south on scenic Hwy 101, seeing the cliffs drop away to the ocean below as they followed the Oregon coastline. Next stop was at Cannon Beach, where students had the opportunity to snap photos of the iconic Haystack Rock and hear a mini-lecture on tsunami planning initiatives in Pacific coastal communities.

Continuing south, the group stopped to visit the Umpqua Dunes—a rolling desert of 4,000 acres that extends three miles inland from the ocean. We received a great photo from Mackenzie later that evening, showing the group laughing and having fun jumping from the top of the dunes into the soft sand below.

Coos Bay

Their final destination was Coos Bay where they spent the next two days staying at the Oregon Institute of Marine Biology (OIMB) exploring and learning about marine life found in tidal pools, exploring the rocky inter-tidal zone in Cape Arago National Park, and hearing about the difficulties of wetland restoration at the South Slough, the first National Estuarine Reserve.

You may be thinking by now that this field experience was crammed with activity. It was—the entire trip took eight days. From Coos Bay, the group returned to Portland to fly back to Boston.

Cutting loose at the Umpqua Dunes

Grand Isle, Louisiana

After being back at Mystic for a short time, Mackenzie and his class flew to New Orleans for place-based learning that was part of the Louisiana Field Seminar. This was the group's last seminar for the semester. It introduced students to the complexity of the environmental and political issues that exist in southern Louisiana due to the erosion of the coastline, as well as the rising water which impacts the Mississippi River Delta and the Gulf Coast. For most of the seminar, Mackenzie and the rest of his class lived at the Louisiana Universities Marine Consortium (LUMCON), an innovative scientific and educational facility located directly on the marsh. He observed firsthand the impact of sea-level rise on nature, and heard from locals about the impact on their livelihood and lives. He learned from an expert at LUMCON about the sedimentary dynamics of deltas and wetlands.

In Grand Isle, located on Louisiana's only inhabited barrier island, both the mayor and town supervisor spoke to the class about the impact of flooding and storms on the community. In addition, they discussed the impact on the island of the 2010 Deepwater Horizon Oil Spill in the Gulf of Mexico. Four million barrels of oil spilled into the Gulf, poisoning marine life and suffocating the shore with tar. Previously, Hurricanes Katrina and Rita had devastated the island.

Biloxi-Chitimacha-Choctaw Indians

The group traveled to Dulac, where they met Chief Shirell Parfait-Dardar of the Grand Caillou/Dulac Band of Biloxi-Chitimacha-Choctaw Indians. She shared how erosion and flooding threatened her tribe's way of life. For 20 years, the tribe had been fighting for federal tribal recognition which had complicated their efforts to prepare for a changing climate. By not being recognized, the tribe did not qualify for government aid that was desperately needed to address the issues impacting the community and surrounding area.

The Chief also took the group to see the graves of her people. They were completely above-ground, having been uprooted by hurricanes and storms that had washed away the earth exposing the graves. This experience had a defining impact on Mackenzie's thoughts, research, and college studies.

To balance out the serious studies, there was time allotted for students to experience the rich Cajun culture of Louisiana. Mackenzie had fun along with the rest of the group at a crawfish boil, which consisted of crawfish, sausage, baked potatoes, corn, and mushrooms. They danced the two-step to fiddle music and had the opportunity to fish in the river while alligators lurked nearby.

With a lasting impression of the 3-day Louisiana Field Seminar, the group flew back to Boston and returned to Mystic Seaport where they would remain for the rest of the semester.

Moot Court

Mackenzie spent April attending classes, doing independent research, working, and developing his maritime skill by building a small kayak with three other classmates. April was also the month when family members were invited for a Family Day at Mystic Seaport to see students' work featured in person.

I decided to attend the weekend event along with my sister who, as you may recall, lived in Boston. The visit provided the opportunity to see where Mackenzie was living and learning. At the same time, I used the opportunity to interview a few students attending colleges in Boston as part of my research for this book. I was interested in learning about their college experiences and how they compared to those of gap year students I had interviewed.

"Students carry with them the baggage that they carry into college…..A large number struggle with anxiety and depression and other mental health issues. I think that our society and culture have placed too much pressure on students, especially those who are driven to excel. High achievers. I deal with a lot of perfectionism and concerns about the grade. One of the wonderful things that does happen here often is that students eventually begin to learn to love learning vs. focusing on the grade."

Williams-Mystic Executive Director, Tom Van Winkle, Ph.D.

When we arrived for Family Day, I learned that Mackenzie and his classmates had just completed Moot Court—a week-long experience where they had prepared arguments and presented them to a real-life judge, Derek Langhauser, Attorney and Chief Counsel to the Governor of Maine. The students' case was a landmark beach access case known as the Moody Beach case, which had been litigated in Maine. The experience focused not only on constitutional law but also illustrated to students what it meant to make laws and what happened when individuals in charge of making laws went in different directions.

When I met the faculty member who oversaw the Moot Court experience, she was glowing in her remarks about Mackenzie. She said that the judge who presided over the court had been impressed with both the way his mind worked and the argument he used to present his case. Judge Langhauser had said that anytime Mackenzie would like an internship, he would hire him. He must take after my sister the attorney, I am thinking.

A proud Mom moment, of course. It was heartwarming to hear this feedback about Mackenzie from one of his faculty members. It was particularly meaningful because she had been one of two faculty members who had been against admitting Mackenzie into the program, according to Tom Van Winkle, the program ED. Both faculty members had expressed their concerns that he would not be able to handle the academics taught at a junior and senior college level.

He proved them wrong!

What was noticeable to me during Family Day was the sense of community, feelings of trust, and pride for the learning that students had

Examining marine life

gained from the program. I left knowing that Mackenzie would take away tremendous knowledge from his experience at Williams-Mystic.

In May, Mackenzie wrapped up his semester by presenting his independent research and finishing his final exams. After saying sad farewells to his classmates and instructors, he caught a ride to the Boston airport where he boarded a plane to return home to Portland. The last 17 weeks had afforded him the opportunity to begin the transition to being a college student, albeit not a traditional start, but still a step toward returning to a learning environment that would be heavily focused on classroom instruction.

More importantly, I knew he was ready for college.

I wondered, though, what would his college experience be like now that he'd had two more years to mature. Would he retain his renewed sense of curiosity as he enters college and experiences learning in a traditional classroom environment?

> "I lived outside of my comfort zone throughout the semester and I feel like I could do anything because of it. It really taught me that you should say yes to every opportunity you are given because you never know what will become of it. I tell people all the time, don't lock doors you haven't even tried opening yet."
> — Williams Mystic Blog

Mackenzie's 2nd Gap Year Plan

May - June
- WORK + save $ for AT hike
- Prepare for hike
- + Family decision - move to PDX. Trip to PDX.

June
- Drive to Harpers Ferry with ~~Mom~~, Dad, + Stuart
- Begin AT northbound solo hike ~~with Mom, Dad, + Stuart~~

July - September
- Continue solo hike northbound. Resupply/3days
- Summit Mt. Katahdin - AT northern terminus
- Return to Harpers Ferry
- + 2 week Break - Visit friends Boston + Tampa

~~September~~ October - December
- Begin southbound solo hike at Harpers Ferry
- Complete thru hike of AT - Springer Mtn, GA
- ~~Return to Nazzy~~ Travel to PDX

December - January
- Apply to colleges
- • ~~Find job in Nazzy~~ PDX. Save $ for college.
- + ~~Apply/~~Accept admission to Williams-Mystic Semester.
  - + Start Jan. Fly to Boston.
    Aunt/uncle drop off at
    Mystic Seaport.

~~February - August~~ Jan - May
- • ~~WORK~~ Complete Williams-Mystic
- • Make college decision
- • ~~Begin college~~ Return to PDX

May - ~~August~~
- • ~~Get job.~~ WORK - Save $ for college.
- • Begin College

What You Can Do

1. Check in with your young adult about their thoughts and readiness of returning to a classroom environment.
2. Discuss with your young adult the impact their time away may have on their approach to college.
3. Allow your young adult to pursue activities that will help them learn and grow without interference.

Notes

Am I Too Late?

Chapter 12
Quack Mack Goes To Ducktown

You don't have to see the whole staircase, just take the first step.
—Martin Luther King

A child's creativity never ceases to amaze me.

As a farewell gift from Williams-Mystic, Mackenzie received an illustrated children's book, *Quack Mack Goes To Ducktown*. Written by one of Mackenzie's favorite faculty members and illustrated by his 8-year-old daughter, the story is about Mackenzie's time at Williams-Mystic.

You can probably guess: Quack Mack refers to Mackenzie. His name was shortened to Mack by many of the Williams-Mystic faculty and Tom Van Winkle early on in the semester. It seemed only fitting that this nickname be used in the book, because it handily rhymed with "quack," a sound most associated with a duck.

Even more fitting is the fact that the Williams-Mystic program is centered around the study of water, and there are many ducks around Mystic Seaport. Creating Mackenzie in the image of a duck was very cleverly done by this 8-year-old.

At the end of the book, you see Quack Mack ready to say goodbye. He has made his college decision and is ready to go.

I'm going to college!

Deja vu

Mackenzie's original plan, after hiking the AT, was to use December and January to apply for colleges and universities. Another college search (yikes)! This time, however, he had a much shorter list, and also had just a couple of weeks for the search before he departed for the Williams-Mystic semester. Once he departed for New England, he knew there would be little time to work on a college search.

Mackenzie focused his efforts on applying to a handful of public and private colleges and universities in Oregon and California since we now resided in the Pacific Northwest. Attending a public university in Oregon was the more affordable option for him. Because of Mike's education benefit as a state employee, Mackenzie would qualify for reduced tuition and pay only 30% of tuition costs for 12 hours each term. This would be a significant savings for us in paying for college, particularly, since we were living on only one income again.

Mackenzie submitted applications to the University of Oregon, the University of Oregon Clark Honors College, and Oregon State University.

Believing there was a chance that private colleges might offer him a strong financial aid package, Mackenzie also applied to Willamette University, Pomona College, and Stanford.

I wish I could say that the second time around was easier, but I can't. On our trip returning from California after the holidays, I was concerned to see Mackenzie exhibiting behavior that I had observed during his senior year of high school. He was becoming anxious as he engaged in his college search. When I shared my concerns with him, I broke down in tears. It was heartbreaking to see that he was trapped into believing that college would forever define him. Mackenzie recognized that he had jumped back on the treadmill again. He said that he was compelled to apply to schools that his peers were attending, like Stanford, because of his drive to compete.

You can imagine his excitement, then, when he heard back from a Stanford alum from Nashville about setting up an alumni interview. He had made it one step further in the admission process than when he applied in high school! Because Mackenzie's college application materials were on file at USN and reflected a Nashville address, Stanford's Admissions Office assumed he was still living in Tennessee and connected him to an alum living in Nashville.

This would be one of a number of challenges that Mackenzie would face in applying to colleges almost two years after high school graduation. Admissions offices at many of the top universities and colleges that primarily enroll traditional-age students are not set up to handle applications from someone with alternative experiences like Mackenzie.

Once the initial confusion was cleared up, Mackenzie enjoyed his conversation with the alum. He told Mike and me after the call that she had been very positive. She said he would be a wonderful addition to Stanford but she did not make the admissions' decision. She also told him that any college would be lucky to have him. I was very appreciative that this alum had reinforced the idea that he would be okay wherever he went to school. His chances of being admitted to Stanford were slim, due to the number of applications they received every year and their acceptance rate of 4.5%.

While he was away studying in the Williams-Mystic Program, Mackenzie received notification of admission decisions from the colleges to which he had applied. Of the six schools, he had been admitted into all of them but

Pomona and Stanford. As before, May 1st was Mackenzie's deadline for choosing the school he wanted to attend.

Affordability was a big factor to consider. Willamette University had provided a generous financial aid package that included merit scholarships, which made attending a small private college an option. However, the more affordable option would be to attend one of the state institutions where, through enrollment in the Honors College, he could pursue studies in an environment similar to one found at a selective private college or university. In order to compete for bright, academically-focused students, a number of public universities across the US have established Honors Colleges. Both the University of Oregon and Oregon State offer an Honors College option which was a factor in Mackenzie's decision to apply to these two schools.

Learning to navigate systems

Unfortunately, when Mackenzie received his acceptance letters in April, both the University of Oregon and Oregon State had admitted him as a transfer student. This admissions' decision knocked him out of consideration for scholarships generally awarded to entering freshmen. This was confusing, because he had not started college.

So why was he considered a transfer student?

The answer lies in the fact that these college admissions offices were not equipped to receive an application like Mackenzie's that included alternative learning experiences that had occurred after high school. As part of his application, Mackenzie was required to report previous or current enrollment at other educational institutions. Since he was enrolled in a semester program through Williams College, Mackenzie shared this information on his college applications, not realizing the impact this would have on the admissions decision.

Because he reported that he had been enrolled elsewhere, the admissions offices at UO and OSU deemed him a transfer student. They failed to recognize that Mackenzie was not enrolled in a degree program at Williams College nor was he seeking academic credit. The Williams-Mystic program was a stand-alone program, similar to a structured program offered through a gap year provider, which students do not report unless they are seeking credit.

In hindsight, it would have been better if he had not reported his studies through Williams-Mystic because it took a lot of effort to clear up this issue. Like most colleges, UO and OSU admissions offices and their application processes were designed for traditional applicants or for students transferring from an Oregon community college. Mackenzie's alternative experiences, including NOLS and Williams-Mystic, did not fit the traditional student profile. Because he had reported these experiences, Mackenzie was determined by the admissions offices of both schools to be a transfer student, which disqualified him from being eligible for freshmen scholarships.

Dealing with the bureaucracy of the different schools was quite frustrating for him. However, in the end, things worked out. He would later transfer his credits from Williams-Mystic and apply them to his Environmental Studies major. The money he saved from not paying tuition for these credits was worth more than the scholarships he would have received.

Out-of-state or in-state student?

To make it even more confusing, one of the schools admitted him as an "out-of-state" student, while the other school admitted him as an "in-state" student.

Why?

When Mackenzie applied to schools in January, he had to submit information that had been compiled for college applications two years before at USN, his Tennessee high school. As happened with Stanford, the assumption was made that Mackenzie was still living in Tennessee. It's not clear why this continued to be a mistake because he had used his new home address in Portland when applying. This is a clear example where systems were not integrated within the admissions processes at the universities where he applied.

After a good deal of back and forth between admissions and financial aid offices at both UO and OSU, Mackenzie was able to resolve the issues related to out-of-state status and clear up the confusion regarding the Williams-Mystic program. It had been a painful and stressful process trying to navigate these issues while also participating in the Williams-

Mystic program. He was taking classes at the junior and senior college levels, and was working hard to have a strong finish to the semester.

Ultimately, Mackenzie made the decision to enroll at the University of Oregon Clark Honors College. When looking at his different options, it seemed to make the most sense. UO offered strong environmental science and environmental studies programs—both of interest to him. The Honors College provided him an opportunity to be a member of a smaller cohort of students on campus who sought to be challenged intellectually and academically. It was also affordable due to Mike's education benefit.

Sticker shock!

In looking at the overall costs to attend, however, I was shocked at how expensive it would be to attend UO for a year. If Mackenzie had not been eligible for the education benefit through Mike's employer, his cost to attend UO for one year would have been more than $29,000, which was slightly less than a year at Willamette University, a private school. As it was, we were on the hook for approximately $24,000 (yes—that is one year at a state school) of which $13,400 covered housing and meals for the three terms. All public universities in Oregon are on a quarter system which is equivalent to a fall and spring semester.

And the housing costs blew me away. UO had made the decision to require all first-year students to live on campus in one of its residence halls, and the policy was being implemented Mackenzie's first year. Like many universities, UO had been in the process of upgrading its residential housing communities to attract students. That meant it needed a way to pay for the upgrades, hence the decision for all first-year students to live on campus. To reduce his housing cost, Mackenzie applied to live in the Global Scholars Hall in a triple. If he hadn't, his housing costs would have been closer to $15,000 for nine months.

Once I got over the sticker shock of the cost to attend four years at UO, I embraced the sense of relief. Mackenzie would be "going off to college" in the fall—much more prepared for his college studies than two years before.

Finally a Duck

Those of you unfamiliar with the University of Oregon may not know that their mascot is a duck—they are the Oregon Ducks.

On campus and in the community, there is no shortage of jokes and references about ducks. For instance, you may see someone wearing a tee-shirt on campus that says "Addicted to Quack," or a Darth Vader reference like "Join the Duck Side."

It was not surprising when Mackenzie had to attend a two-day orientation on campus called: "Introducktion." To be honest, some of these jokes really "quacked" us up.

When Mackenzie received the communication from UO that he was "required" to sign up for orientation, he was annoyed. UO had been clear that it would grant only a few exceptions for not attending. This meant that he would miss two days of work (and income) because orientation dates were scheduled during the work week. Mackenzie was not sure how his request to take time off during a peak work season would be received. You can understand his fears because we all have been in his shoes at one time in our lives—starting a job and proving yourself is not easy.

Woes of the working student

Mackenzie began to search for a job immediately when he returned to Portland from Williams-Mystic. After three weeks of actively looking, he landed a job as a camp counselor for Mazama's Adventure Wild Camp—a day camp in Portland, that ran weekly programs for eight weeks over the summer, beginning mid-June and ending early August. The job would not start for four weeks, so he accepted a second job working the graveyard shift at a donut shop. His plan was to work hard, prove himself and negotiate with them to just work weekends when he started the camp job (remember, one of his strengths is "woo").

That plan didn't work out.

After four weeks at the donut shop, he ended up quitting because there was little flexibility and support from his manager. He had fallen ill and the expectation was that he show up to work even if he was sick.

The timing worked out, however. The following week, Mackenzie started his camp job, which was a great fit. He enjoyed being outside and overseeing the activities of eight to ten pre-school age children.

To ensure he could attend orientation at UO in late July, Mackenzie had arranged to take two days off in advance of starting his job at the camp. He wanted to give as much advance notice to the camp director so she would not be left short-handed when he was absent.

Parents were also invited to attend Introducktion, so I decided to join Mackenzie for one of the two days he was scheduled to attend. The university offered a number of sessions for parents on topics like financial aid and health and safety. I was a little curious about the session on "Letting go" and the advice UO would provide parents. From my firsthand experience working at Vanderbilt, I had found that many parents of college students struggled with this and were often overly involved in their students' lives. For me, Mackenzie had "left the nest" when he departed for NOLS two years before, and Mike and I had worked hard to support his launch without (much) interference.

Joining the flock

During orientation, Mackenzie and I saw little of each other. He was assigned to a "flock," a group of students, led by two upperclass students, that were together over the two-day orientation (yes, UO really really likes its Duck!). The primary purpose of the small groups was to help students develop some connections before coming to campus in the fall.

Orientation was also the time when students enrolled in their fall classes. Upon arrival to Introducktion, students were assigned a time to meet one-on-one with an academic advisor to discuss fall term classes, after which they were asked to go online and register for classes. Due to the number of students needing advising, appointments were spread out over the two-day orientation. To Mackenzie's dismay, he had been assigned the last slot on the last day which meant there was a strong likelihood that classes he wanted would be full.

And that is exactly what happened. He was not able to enroll in ANY of the classes he had selected in consultation with his advisor. After leaving his advising session, Mackenzie went to the library to log-on to the system to register. When he couldn't register for any of the classes because they were full, he did not know what to do. So he went back to where he had met his Advisor but they were gone. Then he tried reaching someone at the Honors College to get guidance, they had left for the day as well. Remember, he had been one of the last group of students to be scheduled at the end of the second day.

Having been unable to register, Mackenzie discussed what his options might be as we drove home. I was struck by the impact this had had on him.

Mackenzie had not even started UO, and already the system of advising was curtailing his enthusiasm for studying topics of interest and having him default to subjects that were needed to fulfill college and university requirements.

But, it did not end up all bad.

As a Clark Honors College student, he was expected to enroll in one of the college's introductory seminars. There were two seminars available to him that were not full, so he decided to enroll in "Poetry and You," taught by Dr. Barbara Mossberg (aka Dr. B). By a stroke of luck, Mackenzie was inspired and challenged by her during his first term, and she became a wonderful mentor to him during his time at UO.

College freshman

Late September arrived and Mackenzie's first year began. His experience was a lot like other first-year students experience at many colleges and universities across the US. He lived in a residence hall with a couple of freshman roommates, took classes—some through the Honors College and others through the College of Arts and Science.

He engaged in activities outside of school: he joined the Climbing Club and the Outdoor Recreation leadership program, volunteered for the Adaptive Ski Program, and attended a few sporting events. During his first year, Mackenzie was fortunate to have mentors who were eager to challenge and support him in his learning journey that included exploring women and gender studies, poetry, and glacier studies.

Mackenzie also earned one of two undergraduate spots in the Glacier Research Lab headed by Dr. Mark Carey, and applied for and received an

Move-in day

environmental justice scholarship that covered part of his tuition for the next year. Being "out of the classroom" did not seem to have negatively impacted his ability to apply himself inside and outside the classroom. His first year was full.

Before finals were done in June, Mackenzie moved back home and finished his finals remotely. Stuart was graduating from high school, and Mackenzie wanted to take part in the celebration activities. He also started back at Adventure Wild Camp for another summer working as a Camp Counselor. Pretty amazing focus.

And then....

One morning in August, Mike and I were enjoying a Sunday brunch out on our deck, when Mackenzie came outside and asked if he could join us. He had an idea that he wanted to float by us to see what we thought. We immediately knew something was up. If you remember, one of Mackenzie's greatest strengths or "superpowers" is his "woo." He has the ability to win over others to his ideas and way of thinking by the way he communicates.

"What would you think if I took off the fall term from UO and went to France with Stuart?" Mackenzie asked.

Stuart, like Mackenzie, had decided to take a gap year before starting college and did not yet have a plan for the fall.

Mackenzie went on to say that the two of them had been talking with my nephew Chris (who was staying with us at the time) about becoming a 'fellowship of three' and spending the fall in France. Yes, my sons are Lord of the Ring fans! Mackenzie suggested that this would be good for Stuart since he did not have a plan for the fall and that it would help him socially to travel and live with people he knew.

Mackenzie continued on with his "sales" pitch. He wanted to be able to solidify his French language skills. After taking French for seven years in school, he was still not able to carry on a conversation. He felt that three months in France, where he would be immersed in the language, would help. He also wanted to get a job WWOOFing. It was one of the things on his gap year bucket list that he had not done.

What is WWOOFing?

To be a WWOOFer means to live and volunteer on an organic farm or property that is part of the WWOOF (World Wide Opportunities on Organic Farms) network of national organizations across the globe.[84] Volunteers usually work four to six hours a day in exchange for board, room, and the opportunity to learn about sustainability practices from the host. Being a WWOOFer is one of the activities a number of gap year students choose to do because it is an affordable option for living and working abroad or in the US.

As you can imagine, we had lots of questions once Mackenzie floated one of his famous "trial balloons" by us.

What would this do for his scholarships? Would the university support a leave of absence? What would this mean for his housing? He had signed a 9-month lease on a house with two other roommates. How would he fund the costs of three months in France? What did he hope to learn from this experience? And, more importantly, could he pay for it? We were not willing to invest funds to cover costs for this alternative plan.

Chris had offered to purchase tickets for both Stuart and Mackenzie using airline miles that he had accrued. They would each pay for their own return flight and share the expenses of food, lodging, and other travel costs.

It did not take us long to recognize that there was value in Mackenzie's taking the fall term off if he could work out the details with UO and his roommates. His plan actually provided a solution for something I had been concerned about—Stuart's lack of a defined fall experience for his gap year plan. For the spring, he had signed up for a three-month gap year program through *Where There Be Dragons*, where he would be living and learning in Nepal. Interestingly enough, we learned later that this was the same organization that Malia Obama enrolled in for her gap year.

I felt that Stuart would be better off if he were not living at home for the fall because he needed to begin building his independence. Apparently, Mike was worried too. Until Mackenzie recognized our concerns and suggested the trip to France, we hadn't realized that we were both feeling that Stuart needed to be engaged in something outside of Portland. We just did not know what.

Mike and I gave our support with the understanding that Mackenzie would need to confirm that he could take a leave of absence from school without it adversely affecting his scholarships and position at the Honors College. Not surprisingly, Mackenzie was able to secure all the permissions and approvals from roommates and university officials to move forward with his plan to go to France in the fall.

Off to France

Late September arrived, and once again Mike and I were dropping Mackenzie and his backpack off at the airport (along with Stuart and Chris) for another learning journey that involved living in France for three months—continuing his unorthodox college experience.

Lots of learning occurred during those three months. This included learning how to navigate daily challenges of traveling with two other individuals. For example, the first night they arrived in France, they found out the Airbnb reservation in Paris was a scam, so they had to problem-solve and come up with a solution that they were all willing to

WWOOFing in France

get behind. As you know, it is often hard enough to get one other person on the same page while traveling, let alone a second person. There was a lot of negotiation that occurred over the three months.

One of the highlights for Mackenzie was living and working for a month on an organic olive farm in the south of France near Nimes. He also had the opportunity to hike in the Alps near Chamonix, camp in the beautiful Fontainbleu forest, and see the winter lights of Lyon. And, of course, he spent three weeks in Paris, absorbing the culture and experiencing the history of this wonderful city.

Did he become fluent in French by the end? Not fully, but he gained enough fluency to be able to carry on conversations with the parents of his host on the olive farm who did not speak any English. That was an accomplishment he was proud of. And the entire cost for this experience was $2,500.

In late December, Mackenzie departed Paris along with Chris and Stuart, and flew back to the US having created memories for a lifetime. The 'fellowship of three' had forged an incredibly close relationship—cemented by the experience of living, learning, working, and navigating the unknown together.

Back at school for winter term, Mackenzie focused on academics and completing his application for the prestigious Ernest F. Hollings Undergraduate Scholarship offered by the National Oceanic and Atmospheric Administration (NOAA.)[85] He had set a goal to compete for a national scholarship or fellowship while at UO, and the deadline for the Hollings Scholarship was the first week of February. If selected as a Hollings Scholar, Mackenzie would receive up to $19,000 of academic assistance over two years and a 10-week, full-time, paid summer internship at a NOAA research facility of his choosing. It would provide him an incredible opportunity to engage in hands-on science research, as well as technology, policy, management, and education activities. Additionally, he would develop connections with professionals who could help him with future job prospects after college.

For his application, Mackenzie proposed to research tidewater glaciers—glaciers that feed into the ocean—in Alaska, a perfect fit for his interests. With the help of his faculty mentors (and Mike, who is an excellent proofreader), Mackenzie was able to meet the application deadline.

On a roll, he also applied for and received an undergraduate research award for the summer (offered through UO) and was hired to be a student advisor in the Environmental Studies Department.

Life throws a curveball

In March, Mackenzie and I met for a ski day at Mt. Hoodoo—a little ski area not far from Bend, Oregon. I noticed right away that he was visibly sick, not just with a short-term illness but something more serious.

The previous year, when Mackenzie first returned to Portland from the AT, I felt intuitively that something was not right. I was observing fatigue, lethargy, and brain fog in him. Five months later, I became even more concerned when he returned from his semester at Williams-Mystic and fell ill the third day after starting his job at the donut shop working the graveyard shift. He continued to work for three more weeks, before quitting, because the manager expected him to work even while sick.

It was during his last week at the donut shop when I suggested that he schedule an appointment to see his primary care physician and explore why he was not feeling well. Mackenzie scheduled a visit and was tested for mono and other conditions, but nothing was revealed. A friend of mine, a savvy massage therapist, suggested that Mackenzie be tested for Lyme disease. She noted that Lyme disease could be at play with his history as an AT thru-hiker. It's amazing what massage therapists know about the body and illnesses!

When I shared her suggestion with Mackenzie, he did what most 19-year-olds do—he ignored it. However, a chance encounter a few weeks later, led Mackenzie to take action. He was hiking with Stuart on a short section of the Pacific Crest Trail when they met another hiker, Eowyn (her trail name). She described her journey of living with and recovering from Lyme disease. When Mackenzie described his symptoms, Eowyn encouraged him to be tested for Lyme. She told him there was a national database he could search to identify a doctor who specializes in the treatment of Lyme.

This time, Mackenzie took action. He located a doctor in Portland and scheduled an appointment. After the initial consultation and subsequent testing, Mackenzie received a diagnosis of "acute Lyme disease." This news came just three weeks before he was to start his first year at UO.

The impact of Lyme disease

Lyme disease is the fifth most reported disease in the US. Transmission of the bacteria leading to Lyme comes from deer ticks found in more than 43 of the 50 states in the US.[86] If caught early, in the first three weeks of infection, the prognosis for recovery is good. However, when there is a delay in treatment, like in Mackenzie's case, it is often debilitating to those infected with symptoms that include chronic fatigue, joint stiffness and pain, cognitive decline, unexplained pain, and mood changes (irritability, anxiety, and depression).

Mackenzie likely contracted the disease while hiking the AT. According to his doctor, (a specialist in treating Lyme), white-footed mice carry Borrelia Burgdorferi (Lyme disease) in their bodies. They are then bitten by ticks who ingest Borrelia while feeding on the mice. The ticks then detach from the mice and bite humans transmitting the disease.[87] Mackenzie doesn't remember getting a tick bite. However, he told me one of the things that had been the hardest for him to get used to while hiking the AT was having the mice running across his face at night when he slept in the shelters. I still shudder at this visual.

Like most young people, particularly those in college, Mackenzie did not consistently follow the treatment protocol that his doctor gave him. He had always been physically and mentally strong (which was how he had been able to power through a year-and-a half of school, work, and a trip to France). However, by spring, the disease had caught up with him and was impacting his ability to concentrate and focus. He had pain in his body in different places and was frustrated by not feeling well. He was no longer sure of his purpose for being in school and was struggling with brain fog.

I thought Mackenzie might just drop out of college at this point, but he hung in through the spring term and finished with a strong academic performance. He received word in April that he had been awarded the prestigious Hollings Scholarship through NOAA and was excited about what this would mean for him in the short-term. The financial award, itself, would cover all his expenses for the next two years at UO!

Mackenzie moved home for the summer and returned a third year to work at Adventure Wild Summer Camp. He lasted three days before he came home one night and said he wanted to quit. He felt he was failing the campers because he did not have the energy or patience to be with young children outside all day long. It was too taxing on him physically. This was the same person who had hiked 30 miles each day carrying a 30 pound pack on the AT!

My grown son, who had never been one to cry, broke down in tears. Mike, Stuart, and I circled around him and just held on. It was the turning point for Mackenzie. He recognized that he could no longer avoid addressing his illness. It would require creating a plan and taking action for him to exert control over living with a chronic health condition. Individuals who suffer from Lyme can regain their health but it requires concentrated effort and time. It would also require him to be vulnerable by sharing his condition with others.

The next day, Mackenzie went to work and spoke to the camp director, sharing with her for the first time that he had Lyme and that it was too hard for him to work full-time. She was very supportive and they both agreed to a schedule where he would work 2 ½ days a week.

Mackenzie sat down with Mike and me, and we discussed how we could support him and helped him think of steps he might want to take moving forward. He wanted to get a second opinion on whether he had Lyme disease. He decided to pursue counseling and planned to set up a care team that included naturopathic and allopathic care, nutrition counseling, and massage therapy.

A second opinion

In early August, Mackenzie met with a second doctor and received the same diagnosis of "acute" Lyme disease. He began following the treatment protocols recommended by his doctor, which included the elimination of gluten, dairy, and refined sugar from his diet. Mackenzie had already made changes to his diet, but renewed his commitment to eating more healthy foods. He did yoga and exercised every day. He also continued to paint and journal—activities that he had found helpful in processing his emotions. He wrote to his faculty mentors and shared with them about having Lyme. This was a huge step in sharing his vulnerability with those individuals whose opinions he valued. Over the previous months he had not been able to follow-through on research and other commitments. By sharing his condition, they would have insight into why.

Mackenzie told me that he shared with one of his mentors that he did not regret hiking the AT. "The AT gave me so much. But it also took something away."

Healing through meditation

Back to campus

Mackenzie returned to UO for the fall term and enrolled full-time thinking he could manage the workload. Three weeks into the term, I was not surprised when he told Mike and me that he had dropped all his classes but two, "Native Americans and Environmentalism" and a PE class on Tai Chi. He simply was not well enough to focus on studies. Mackenzie knew that this would impact his scholarships including the one from NOAA, but he needed time to improve his overall health, which meant plenty of rest, exercise, and eating healthy.

Mike and I told him that whatever he chose to do, we would support him, even if it meant dropping out of college. Mackenzie did not give up. He stuck out the term and was glad he did because the "Native Americans and Environmentalism" class was one of the "best" classes he took at UO.

In December, Mackenzie contacted NOAA and forfeited the Hollings Scholarship. He had been too late in the fall term to apply for a leave of absence that was required by NOAA to maintain student eligibility. Mackenzie had learned something that many adults struggle with—the

Healing through art

importance of "letting go" of something to "take on" something new. In his case, he needed to focus on his health.

Feeling stronger, Mackenzie enrolled in 12 hours for winter term. One of the classes that had a profound impact on him was "Inside Out," a class on climate justice where he and ten other students and the professor, traveled by van once a week to the Oregon State Penitentiary in Salem, where they had class with ten "inside" (incarcerated) students.

Winter term ended and I was relieved (and proud) that Mackenzie had been able to complete the term without having to drop any classes. Like other college students across the US and abroad, he had finished the term online when the global pandemic led to college closures.

Unlike many of his peers who struggled with the transition, Mackenzie easily adapted to the change. As he moved into the spring term online, he discovered that he enjoyed online learning more than he thought he would. With everything constantly in flux because of COVID-19, Mackenzie participated in his classes remotely from different locations including Eugene, Portland, and Sisters, Oregon. He was able to complete the term successfully from home in June.

Late in the spring term, Mackenzie made the decision to withdraw from the Honors College. It was a decision he struggled with because of the relationships he had forged with faculty mentors in the college. However, the idea of spending a year writing a thesis did not appeal to him—an exercise that was steeped in academic tradition that would have no relevance to or impact on things he cared about. By withdrawing, he was also free to finish early. He would have the option of graduating in the fall, which would save money and time.

Over the summer, I was struck by the difference between the two summers. Mackenzie had regained much of his strength and was making plans to graduate in the fall. To do so meant taking summer classes online. Part of his studies would be an independent research project for a professor involved with Oregon historical markers.

Moving online

Like many other colleges and universities across the country, for the 2020 Fall Term, UO planned to offer students the option of taking classes on campus, in-person, or online. However, after seeing other campuses across the US open up in August resulting in an outbreak of COVID-19 on their campuses, UO changed directions at the last minute and went to offering all classes online. This did not impact Mackenzie, who had already decided in the summer to take classes online for the fall. He was still thinking he might want to graduate at the end of the term, but had not made a final decision.

Pursuing the option to finish, Mackenzie found out that he was required to complete two general education requirements in order to graduate—an entry-level writing course and an entry-level math course. As an Honors College student, Mackenzie had been exempt from taking the general ed (entry-level) writing course. (Honors College classes are writing intensive so students enrolled in the College don't need a separate writing course to fulfill their writing education requirement). However, when Mackenzie withdrew from the Honors College, the university would not allow him to waive the general ed writing requirement.

Upon learning about the two general education requirements, Mackenzie requested consideration for replacing the writing and math courses with upper level courses. And what do you think the university's response was? "Just take the classes."

When Mackenzie told me about the requirements and the university's response to his request, frankly, I was irked. Mackenzie had been covering all his tuition and living expenses because he had worked hard to earn scholarships to cover his costs. However, when he dropped below full-time status due to his illness, he lost his scholarships and was no longer able pay tuition for the fall term. Mike and I agreed to cover tuition but we were on the hook for the full-tuition bill, not a reduced tuition bill (Mike had transitioned from his faculty position at Oregon Tech to an industry position and Mackenzie was no longer eligible to receive the education benefit of 70% off per credit hour).

Mackenzie's experience is yet another example of why higher education needs reform. It would have been better for Mackenzie to take courses on topics that he was curious about, or courses that would better prepare him for what is needed in today's workplace (such as data analytics). Most graduates will never use trig or calculus in their work, so requiring these to graduate makes little sense. It is a waste of money and a questionable investment, considering the cost of tuition.

Final days as a Duck

As I write this chapter, my son will be graduating this December 2020, with a Bachelor of Science degree in Environmental Studies. He is wrapping up his fall term and his undergraduate college experience online from Orcas Island, WA. He moved to the island, located on the Puget Sound, in October to live with a friend who is working as part of a team with AmeriCorp.

Mackenzie will be one of the COVID-19 graduates. What I find amazing is that Mackenzie will have graduated basically in three years and will have zero debt. Because of the tuition break he received, the scholarships he was awarded, and his savings from summer and student employment that he used to pay for college, the total cost for Mackenzie's college degree will be $38,600. Compare this to the $73,400 we would have paid if he had not been so fortunate, or $93,000 if he had completed a fourth year. The investment Mike and I made toward his college education totaled $30,600 which is incredible considering college costs today. And Mackenzie can be proud that he paid for more than half of his college costs because of his efforts to earn scholarships and willingness to work.

	1st year	2nd year	3rd year	Total
Tuition, Fees, Books	$19,300	$11,500	$12,200	$43,000
Room & Board	$13,600	$5,800	$3,200	$22,600
Transportation	$500	$1,400	$1,800	$3,700
Miscellaneous	$2,200	$900	$1,000	$4,100
Total	**$35,600**	**$19,600**	**$18,200**	**$73,400**
Scholarships	($3,000)	($10,400)	($8,600)	($22,000)
Tuition Benefit	($5,400)	($3,800)	($3,600)	($12,800)
Actual cost	**$27,200**	**$5,400**	**$6,000**	**$38,600**

College costs

I would say we were lucky. If Mackenzie had stuck with his original decision to attend the University of Miami, we would have been on the hook for $186, 500, assuming he finished in four years and had maintained at least one scholarship. As you can see from our experience, college is expensive and there are a lot of variables that can impact overall costs, whether you attend a state flagship school or a selective private college.

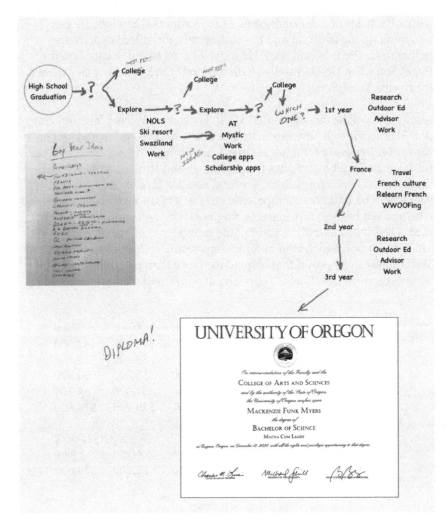

Mackenzie's learning journey

Response Poem to Tennyson's *Ulysses**
By Mackenzie Myers
Fall 2017, University of Oregon Honors College
Poetry and You class with Dr. "B" Mossberg

I cannot rest from travel: I will drink
Life to the lees: All times I have enjoy'd
Greatly, have suffer'd greatly, both with those
That loved me, and alone, on shore, and when
Thro' scudding drifts the rainy Hyades
Vext the dim sea: I am become a name.

That old Tennyson knew what he was talking about

I cannot rest from travel and adventure
It has ingrained itself in the core of my being
A wanderer, a traveler, a nomad, I am and will be
Haunted and blessed by the pull to explore
Yearning with desire to see more and more.

I am a part of all that I have met
This too is true, you wise poet you.
Each new person, new place, new activity
Or experience has imparted upon me
Lessons and Wisdom, forever changing who I will be.

Born in the City above the Clouds
Colorado gave me a deep appreciation
For mountains – with wonder I absorbed
Their splendor, stoicism, and rugged look
Understanding I could not experience life in the confines of a
book.

Uprooted and confused, ready to learn more
Australia gave me a taste of the open road.
I learned to let go, to move on, to live simply
Each day an opportunity to experience something cool
Realizing most knowledge does not come in the form of school.

221

The scudding drifts and vexing currents of the sea
Come next, with Florida imparting on me
An awe for broad seas and the ceaseless toil
Of the Ocean. For its constant hum
A rhythmic, pulsing, all-encompassing drum.

Tennessee gave me solidity, friendship,
Humid summer nights spent exploring,
A love for food, music, hospitality.
The memory of lush, rolling green hills
In the Southeast's crowning jewel, Nashville.

Hiking gave me confidence, courage
A new appreciation for the flow of time.
Walking through Appalachia left its mark
With a Tick's infection coursing in my blood
And wistfulness for my journey periodically crashing like a flood.

I cannot rest from travel: I will drink
Life to the lees: I am become a name.

Friends of mine often do not understand me
For they have not seen what my eyes have seen.
Their Universe has not changed for eternity
While mine constantly shifts at the blink of an eye.
Though I must reconcile, accept their view, this I will try.

Like King Ulysses and his son
Blameless are those who cannot understand
A life not filled with comfort, security, and the familiar.
Who do not dream during class of open roads and the smell of
pine.
In Tennyson's words, they will work their work, I mine.

There lies the port, the vessel puffs her sail:
There gloom the dark, broad seas.

Ulysses, as I do, revels in the power of the ocean.
I dream to sail beyond the sunset, seeking
Understanding of myself.
To follow knowledge like a sinking star
And roam the dark gloomy seas, wide and far.

Mountains I will climb too, both
Towering pinnacles of granite in this world
And mountains contained within my soul.
Not a conqueror will I be of mountains, but a collaborator
Speaking on behalf of the mountain and creatures there, much
like a satyr.

To my fellow comrades, adventurers, travelers, and dreamers
Come, my friends, T'is not too late
We must sail into the sunset, in the pursuit
Of a better world.
Only then can our masts, at last, be furled.

I will not rest from travel: I will drink
Life to the lees. I may suffer greatly, both
With those who love me, and alone.
To strive, to seek, to find, and not to yield.
I keep my eyes always upon the broad seas and open fields.

---

*Part of text adopted from original poem written in by Alfred Lord
Tennyson.[88]

What You Can Do

1. Understand the guidelines and procedures necessary for your young adult to start college after a gap year.
2. Ask your young adult to name a time in their life when they've had to be resilient. Discuss the ways this may or may not have prepared them to deal with life's uncertainty.
3. Discuss with your young adult how the pandemic has affected their learning.

Notes

Chapter 13
Lessons Learned

Education must enable one to sift and weigh evidence, to discern the true from the false, the real from the unreal, and the facts from the fiction.

—Martin Luther King, Jr.

We started this journey in 2015, because what we were doing wasn't working for Mackenzie. He knew it, and after a while, we knew it.

What came next spun all of us into an alternate universe that we could have never imagined—one filled with transitions, new relationships, locations, setbacks, victories, and excitement.

Now, (drum roll, please) Mackenzie is officially a college graduate! Not only that, but he graduated in three years.

Education versus learning

Our goal, originally, was to get him into the best college so he could graduate and be successful in life—a simple plan, but life is not linear. We later discovered there are many ways to achieve this accomplishment. Planning, strategy, and just plain old good luck play a part in the journey. It doesn't have to be four years and out.

Some people use education and learning interchangeably, but we have discovered they are very different. Education seems to be the inflexible system—four years, credits, majors, football teams, spring break, Greek Life—that our students enter in hopes of graduating.

Learning takes place everywhere—Kahn Academy, YouTube videos, vacations, jobs, friends, family, gap years, apprenticeships, coding camps —everyone and everything is a teacher.

We have to be a society that demands lifelong learning, so we have to constantly determine what we need to learn and where the best resources are to teach us.

A four-year education alone will not make our children successful

In his book, *Rethinking Success,* J. Douglas Holladay discusses eight essential practices that he says will help readers be successful in work and life:[89]

- know your story
- maintain relationships
- make gratitude a regular practice
- define success and failure
- invite risk into your life
- live an integrated life
- leave a legacy

Our story is not their story

Knowing your story is one of the most powerful chapters in Holladay's book. "Our story is the central show in living a life of meaning and consequences. Not understanding the various dynamics that have shaped your unique narrative puts you at risk to live someone else's story rather than your own."

In the book, he tells the story of Peter Buffett, son of multibillionaire Warren Buffett, who changed course as a sophomore at Stanford when his father announced that he wasn't leaving his fortune to his three children. The young Buffett immediately dropped out of school and moved to New York City to pursue what he thought was important. He later became a successful songwriter and musician writing the film score for the movie blockbuster *Dances with Wolves.*

Buffett said in retrospect: "We are all born into someone else's story."

The challenge is that our students have to create their own stories.

Therein lies the balance, the dance.

We're parents. We know better, right? We're older, wiser, and have been through the storms of life. Our children should listen to us. True. But at some point, they have to take the wheel. They have to own their mistakes and successes.

Failure, the great teacher

Holladay says a necessary trait for success is the ability to be resilient—to bounce back from failure and hardship—to learn from our experiences. As parents, we need to ask: Can our children fail if we don't let them? Can they be resilient if we always bounce back for them? The parents from the Varsity Blues scandal tried this and the results were not good.

The author says "...failure is actually central to success. Just ask Babe Ruth. Yes, he held the major league home run record, and yet he also held the strikeout record."

The real kicker: we can prepare our students for life, but we can't make them be successful. They have to do that for themselves and we have to accept that it won't always be pretty.

When to talk, when to listen

Jim Bellar said he was sitting in his office one afternoon at Vanderbilt when he received a call from a parent flying on a corporate jet. The parent said his son wasn't making the academic and social choices he thought he should make and wanted to know how he could get him to change his behavior. The man talked about his credentials in the business world and how people valued and respected his opinion.

Jim listened intently for several minutes and then told the parent, half jokingly, to have his next door neighbor tell his son the same thing he was trying to tell him. The executive laughed and then agreed with him.

It's a fact; sometimes our students will listen to anyone else but us, even if we have the best information. Was that true for you growing up? Did you always listen to your parents?

Our family made our share of mistakes during this two-year adventure, full of chaos and new ways of thinking. One of the things we did right (most of the time) was—we listened to our son.

By doing so, we learned a few things as a family.

The power of networks and relationships

This book is filled with connections. Most of us know that's the way people get jobs, but it may not occur to us how often we use connections in everyday life.

Kara Bingham, who worked in higher education study abroad for many years, came for a visit and recommended that Mackenzie look at the National Outdoor Leadership School (NOLS).

If I hadn't met and cultivated a relationship with Peter from Swaziland at Vanderbilt, Mackenzie would have not gone there to teach school.

George Flatau, Mackenzie's cross-country coach and one of his favorite teachers at USN in Nashville, provided context and encouragement for him to delay college and hike the Appalachian Trail. "Hiking the AT would be something that I would never regret," Mackenzie recounted after leaving a meeting with him.

Mackenzie learned about the Williams-Mystic Semester Coastal Studies Program through a friend whose sister had graduated from Williams College and saw it in the alumni newsletter.

And there were many family members who opened up their homes, connected us to their connections for places to stay and offered frequent flyer miles for Mackenzie to travel.

Connections and relationships are worth more than money.

Understanding themes and patterns

As parents, we see themes and patterns emerge as our children decide what toys to play with, who their friends are, what they like to do for fun, what makes them afraid, and what makes them happy. Themes and patterns from experiences define us over time.

As a veteran of the career coaching industry, I have given Mackenzie a few assessments over the years, but I might have known these things simply by observing and asking him questions. I did both.

He has always had a theme of nature and the outdoors. When he was an infant, we lived in the foothills of Pikes Peak in Colorado Springs with nature right outside our back door. As an infant, he observed this world from a backpack when we hiked this beautiful terrain.

When he started Montessori school, Mackenzie had the opportunity to be outside several times a day and benefitted greatly from the Montessori approach of experiential education taught through the senses in the natural world.

He has always enjoyed sports like soccer and cross-country, which helped him understand "finish lines," the importance of staying in good physical shape, and the value of competition, whether it was competing against a team or himself.

When it came to entering the NOLS program, we felt that Mackenzie would not have a problem since nature and competition were in his DNA. The same went for hiking the Appalachian Trail. What we learn in life is cumulative, and Mackenzie had laid the groundwork for these adventures early on.

When he entered the University of Oregon, this pattern continued when he joined the Climbing Club and Outdoor Recreation leadership program, volunteered for the Adaptive Ski Program, became a student advisor for the Environmental Studies Department, and earned a spot in the Glacier Research Lab.

Mackenzie also has a theme of enjoying all kinds of people. According to the assessment StrengthsFinder, one of Mackenzie's top strengths is WOO, which means "winning others over." He has a gift for relationship building, which helped him in all of his gap year adventures from Swaziland to living in France. He has built a strong network, not for personal gain but—because he has no other choice. That's who he is.

Short-term, flexible planning

It's common for organizations to make 10-year plans, only to find they are obsolete or invalid within a few years.

We had a gap year plan, a starting point, but it quickly changed as the circumstances did. Mackenzie had not planned on hiking the AT, going to France, or sailing with the Williams-Mystic program—these were opportunities that presented themselves along the way.

We tried to keep in mind that the experiences were the most important, along with the knowledge and practical skills that he would gain from them.

Adversity and resilience

They say "Shit happens." Right?

Mackenzie was disappointed on the AT when he had a hip injury and had to come off the trail. Later, a giant forrest fire that killed several people blocked his passage. In both cases, he made decisions to adjust and persist.

Much like his gap year plan, things kept changing and he had to change with them. He learned how to adapt, choose alternatives, and move past doubt.

Hiking the Appalachian Trail gave him memories for a lifetime, but it also gave him a tick bite that gave him Lyme Disease, which plagues him to this day. He had to reduce his academic load, go part-time, and let a prestigious national scholarship go, but that did not stop him from getting a college degree in three years.

He was also undeterred when he had to navigate the mysterious world of college admissions—transfer student or not, out of state or in state, and taking classes to fill requirements that couldn't be negotiated to check off a box. All along, he kept his eye on the prize.

Risks and opportunities

Nobody wants to look stupid when trying something new. But life is full of risks.

Mackenzie went to Swaziland by himself at 18 and taught high school English. There were risks from not knowing the language, the culture, the country where AIDS is still prevalent. There were also risks in never having taught before.

He hiked the AT by himself and was given the gift of Lyme Disease as a result.

Each learning journey carried built-in risks, from the physical demands of NOLS to being the only person on the Williams-Mystic voyage who had never been to college.

There is a saying: "No risk, no reward."

A bigger view of the world

During his gap year(s), he came to better understand the importance of sustainable food systems highlighted during his NOLS course and later on from WWOOFing in France.

He encountered social justice issues in Swaziland, a country that is still at the forefront of the battle against AIDS.

While working at Vail Resorts, he observed firsthand the power of employees coming together to advocate for their rights regarding their living spaces. He even attended a company meeting with the Vice President of Human Resources to discuss employee concerns.

He witnessed the effects of global warming firsthand during his Williams-Mystic field experience, and saw how it affects groups like the Biloxi-Chitimacha-Choctaw Indians in Mississippi; he also witnessed the impact of coastal erosion in Grand Isle, Louisiana.

In two years, his learning journey covered three countries and almost half the United States, where he met those who spoke different languages, had different lifestyles, and financial means. Everyone was his teacher.

Skills and competencies

There is a lot of talk today about the value of competency-based education. A competency is simply the ability to do something successfully and efficiently. The Society of Human Resources Management (SHRM) defines them as: "…knowledge, skill, ability or other characteristic (e.g., trait, mindset, attitude), commonly referred to as a KSAO, or a group of characteristics, which, when applied in the appropriate roles, help achieve desired results." [90]

A simpler way to digest this concept is: Skills + Knowledge + Abilities = Competencies.

Most employers want these competencies, but higher education, for the most part, does not have systems in place to teach or measure them. It's little wonder recent graduates have difficulty communicating to employers what they learned in college.

The *Indeed Career Guide* recently identified the "Top 11 Skills Employers Look for in Candidates." [91]

We looked at Mackenzie's learning journeys and indicated the competencies he used in each one.

	Lifeguard	NOLS	Ski resort	Swaziland	AT	Mystic	France	U of O
Communication	✓	✓	✓	✓	✓	✓	✓	✓
Leadership	✓	✓	✓	✓		✓		✓
Teamwork	✓	✓	✓	✓		✓	✓	✓
Interpersonal	✓	✓	✓	✓	✓	✓	✓	✓
Learning/adaptability	✓	✓	✓	✓	✓	✓	✓	✓
Self-management	✓	✓	✓	✓	✓	✓	✓	✓
Organizational	✓	✓	✓	✓	✓	✓	✓	✓
Computer			✓	✓		✓		✓
Problem-solving	✓	✓	✓	✓	✓	✓	✓	✓
Open-mindedness	✓	✓	✓	✓	✓	✓	✓	✓
Strong work ethic	✓	✓	✓	✓	✓	✓	✓	✓

Mackenzie's competencies nourished from each experience

Hands-on career development

Many students rush through college never questioning what they will do when they graduate, so it's not surprising that few use their majors when they go to work. College can be a very expensive career assessment if that was the plan.

After his gap year experiences, Mackenzie said information in the classroom made more sense—it was more relevant. He learned about the needs of others by volunteering, about social justice by living in Swaziland, and about global warming by sailing on the Williams-Mystic. Suddenly issues like social and environmental justice became real. These experiences have informed and shaped him.

According to collegefinance.com, "78% of college graduates participating in a gap year believed the time helped clarify what they wanted to do in life."[92]

Mackenzie's future path is unwritten, but it wouldn't surprise me if social justice and the environment are themes as he moves forward.

Gap year costs

This is probably the area that stresses parents the most. What will it cost me for my student to take time off from school?

The answer is: it all depends.

There is no set price for gap years or learning journeys. For instance, if your student joins AmeriCorps, the costs will be minimal. There are also plenty of scholarships available like the one Mackenzie received from Williams-Mystic. The Gap Year Association has a definition of what a gap year is, but really, it's up to you and your student to determine what this experience will be.

Here is a spreadsheet of our costs for the two years.

| | 1st year | | | 2nd year | |
	NOLS	Ski Resort	Swaziland	AT	Mystic
Tuition, Fees, Books	$13,600	$0	$0	$0	$25,900
Room & Board	$200	$300	$0	$2,000	$7,000
Transportation	$300	$200	$1,900	$500	$800
Miscellaneous	$800	$500	$300	$1,000	$800
Scholarships	$0	$0	$0	$0	$25,700
Income	$0	$1,800	$1,400	$0	$300
Actual cost	$14,900	($800)	$800	$3,500	$8,500

Mackenzie's gap year costs

Will he be successful?

Sometimes Mike and I wonder, after all this song and dance, after all the twists and turns: will Mackenzie be successful in a job or in life?

This is not an easy question for any of us—especially our children–to answer now that the pandemic has upended our lives, systems, and economies around the world.

The pandemic has made many of us stop to take stock of our lives and to ask the tough questions that we've been putting off. What's really important to us? Are we where we thought we would be professionally, personally, financially? How do we want to be remembered?

Mackenzie will have to find his own answers to these questions. We believe he is ready and prepared to do so.

Will he be successful? Only time will tell.

We look to him now to define his own success—to write his own story. We don't know what his future holds, but we do know that we are happy to accompany him on the "trapeze swings" in this crazy circus we call "Life."

Am I Too Late?

Epilogue
A Letter from Mackenzie

Orcas Island, WA
February, 2021

An open letter (to myself, to my teachers, to those who read this book),

Take with you the parts of my writing that speak to you, if any. Leave the rest and forget who I am :)

In recent months, I have become a fan of Dionne Brand, a Canadian poet and writer who explores topics of gender, race, sexuality and feminism. She has influenced my thinking about a number of issues that we face today as a society. I share with you a passage from an essay she wrote last summer that resonated with me at the time and describes how I am feeling right now in my life.

"Everything is up in the air, all narratives for the moment have been blown open — the statues are falling — all the metrics are off, if only briefly. To paraphrase Trouillot, we want 'a life that no narrative could provide, even the best fiction.' The reckoning might be now."[93]

Echoing Dionne Brand in the quote above, despite attempts to get back to "normal" and the way things were before COVID, right now "Everything is up in the air."

I write to you about my "learning journey," my "gap years," decisions and a life I lived from another time, a non-Covid time. But you, and we, live in COVID time. Doors, thrown open, looking towards a future of invention, of better living for all, of restructuring, rethinking, reengaging. A future of creation and love.

Taking gap years, taking "time off," deciding to engage in a learning journey for a little while, was a path that worked really well for me. I met many different people and learned about the world and myself, in ways that would have been difficult to engage for me within a university system and all that it entails. I was able to really choose my interests, choose what decisions or doors I might walk through, choose how to live for myself and approach engaging with others, without a template, for the first time.

When I started attending the University of Oregon, I thought about stopping/quitting/dropping out almost every term beginning my sophomore year. I felt regimented, constrained, and the learning style and class format really weren't meeting me where I was at.

However, looking back, I am glad (and relieved) that I finished college.

Thinking now about online learning, and dovetailing with the limited ability to travel with COVID, the format and function of both "university education" and "gap years", are thrown open. We must rethink everything and change from the Inside Out. Change extending from what we call "education" to how we live our lives, from engaging with others to learning, living in, and relating to this world (Earth).

My advice, taken with a radical grain of salt: Make the decisions about college, about what to do "next", or help your child to do so, that will allow for the most expansive, innovative, and collaborative leaps. Open space to take a "leap of invention", following Frantz Fanon. Perhaps that leap is going to college; perhaps it is another direction entirely.

One aspect that helped me continue my studies was my engagement with the community of Eugene (where the University of Oregon is), as I branched outside of the university community and engaged with the city that I began to enjoy deeply.

Questions I encourage you ask your child since COVID has interrupted the status quo: What does being in community, being in relation to the world and to others look like to you now? And does attending a university or college provide you greater avenues to do this, or does it restrict that movement and connection? Will it expand your worldview, giving you new lenses, or will it constrict them? (Again, COVID times confront all decisions).

238

For parents and students worried about not entering college right away, or what will happen if they do not begin college after high school, take solace in the fact that the university system is not going anywhere at the moment. It's a behemoth of a structure, with billions of billions of dollars invested in it and tied in with distinct policies of settler colonial approaches to land and infrastructure. You have time to live outside the university system, if you are able to and want to, and then enter/re-engage. I recommend *A Third University is Possible* by la paperson and *The Undercommons* by Fred Moten and Stefano Harney as places to begin thinking really critically about what the university/college system is, and what it does, in a U.S. context at least.[94] [95]

Taking some time to prioritize other-than-university life activities, or to just be, may lead you (or your child) down a path you never would have dreamed. Taking a moment to step back, step in, to step out, or swim in a different pond, and then rejoin the university currents if it seems right, may be a leap worth taking for many. But again, all doors are thrown open at this moment.

This freedom of choice is also limited by access, healthcare, diverse backgrounds, and scholarships and financial aid packages from universities and colleges that do not allow for students to keep their award after a gap year, or admissions processes that are dramatically harder to navigate for those not applying directly from high school. This is a facet that requires structural change, particularly in opening up pathways for low-income and marginalized groups to enter college after "time off".

I have no answers for you, only more questions. I am still thinking about the role of the university in my life, and education throughout my entire life.

As I close this letter, I want to say how humbled I am that you have taken an interest in my story. In appreciation and to impart a last few words to ponder, I dedicate the following poem to you:

We live and share this Earth, and must work towards a better future.
We are endlessly creating ourselves,
Together.

I hope you/we
Step through that door
That door of reckoning
Fears and webs of shattered
Dreams
Voices
Washed gently away, transformed
In the doorway

Become who you are
Grow towards the sky
And the Earth
A plant, reaching up
Reaching down
Reaching out and around.

Choosing to make a leap
Perhaps learning, along the way
How to fly.

A Mother's Prayer

*If I had influence with the good fairy who is supposed to preside over
the christening of all children, I should ask that her gift to each child in
the world be a sense of wonder so indestructible that it would last
throughout life, as an unfailing antidote against the boredom and
disenchantments of later years, the sterile preoccupation with things
that are artificial, the alienation from the sources of our strength.*
—Rachel Carson

When Mackenzie was nine months old, he developed croup, a life-threatening condition in infants as the airways in the lungs close and breathing becomes difficult. Recognizing the seriousness of his condition, Mike and I rushed him to the emergency room in the small mountain town near our home. The medicine and treatment did not work, and Mackenzie's condition deteriorated. It was one of the first times as a parent, that I was truly scared. The decision was made to ambulance Mackenzie to a pediatric care unit in a hospital 32 miles away in Colorado Springs.

Details about the nightmarish evening are a blur, but what I do remember is the ride down the winding mountain highway in the back of the ambulance. Seeing my infant son, connected to an IV, oxygen mask over his face, and two paramedics working hard to help him breathe, I prayed.

Being a parent, as many of you know, is an enduring life commitment—full of challenges and rewards. It is hard work and a never-ending dance. As a mother, I have strived to be a "good" Mom. I have been successful at times and have failed at times.

I have advocated for my son when I thought the situation warranted my action. Mike recalls a time when I looked at the med tech who was drawing Mackenzie's blood and told him, "You have one shot." At the time, Mackenzie had had a severe reaction to a sulfa-based antibiotic resulting in vasculitis and was in severe pain. I wanted to be clear to the tech that it was important not to miss.

Throughout the past five years, I have continued to advocate for my son and, despite all the challenges that I have raised in this book regarding the deficiencies of our current K-12 and higher education systems, I am hopeful for our future. COVID-19 has been deadly and has disrupted our educational delivery systems in profound ways. Returning to the status quo, post-pandemic, should not be the path forward.

It's time for change

In closing, I offer a few parting thoughts for parents, high school and college students, college counselors, and college admissions professionals with the belief that "we are not too late" to make a change. There is no time like now.

1. It's time to change the "gap year" name to better reflect this period of time in an individual's life that is not a "gap," but a "learning journey."
2. It's time to replace "student" with "learner" to highlight learning as a lifelong experience. Learning should not stop when an individual graduates from high school or college. See *Long Life Learning* by Michelle Weise.[96]
3. It's time to encourage high school students to pursue affordable options including certificate programs and one or two-year education programs. These represent flexible options in building competencies and essential employability skills. Four-year college is not for everyone. We must remove the "shame" currently associated with these options in today's schools to help address the trillion-plus debt of students.
4. It's time to encourage students to consider alternative higher education options like Wayfinding Academy, a two-year college in Portland, Oregon.[97] Students complete their associates degree in "Self and Society." The experience and curriculum are designed to ensure that students leave with a purpose. Curriculum is focused on developing nine core competencies: wayfinding; understanding self and others; understanding the world; communicating effectively; engaging with information; science, technology, and society; making

good choices; futures and citizenship; and the good life." We need more colleges like Wayfinding Academy in the US!

5. It's time to integrate purpose and meaning-finding as part of the college search process and eliminate the use of college rankings in making college decisions. Rankings have led colleges and parents to act in questionable ways.

6. It's time for colleges and universities to change their current admissions and deferral practices that discourage students from taking time away to explore life and learning experiences before starting college. Systems need to be changed to support these students when they return. There would be no value judgment on the "quality" of students' time-away experiences.

7. It's time to stop the frenzy of college applications and the admissions process during senior year in high school so these students can mentor and lead younger students and enjoy their last year of school.

8. It's time to choose alternative learning experiences that better prepare students for launching as adults. We must not continue to blindly pay college tuition without thought of what will be the return on our investment.

9. It's time for colleges and universities that serve traditional-age college students to encourage applicants to engage in a year of service after high school. These students would be given priority in college admissions decisions.

10. It's time to change the college admissions process to be more equitable to all individuals. Legacy and donor admissions would not be given extra consideration. Test scores should be eliminated in the application process.

A prayer for my son

As I see Mackenzie ready to transition into a new life chapter, I recognize that there will be many life transitions for him. There will be much uncertainty and many highs and lows in his life. The past few years have prepared him well. Since graduating from high school, he has developed a resiliency from his life experiences over the past five years that affords him an ability to adapt to life's uncertainty.

I don't have a crystal ball that allows me to look back to "what might have been" if Mackenzie had gone to college right after high school. But what I can tell you, unequivocally, is that he is not "following the herd." He has chosen a different path.

I look forward to seeing how his life evolves, what he chooses to learn, and what impact he might have as he shares his gifts and leverages his strengths. Michelle Obama, in her bestselling autobiography, does a beautiful job describing how we are always in a constant state of "becoming."[98] She encourages us to think about living a life where we are constantly learning and evolving and in a state of becoming that leads us to our best selves.

As I continue the dance of being Mackenzie's mother, I offer the following prayer for him:

- May you always lean into adversity knowing you will eventually push through.
- May you continue to create and express through your art. There is such beauty in your poetry, writing, and painting.
- May you always have access to nature and draw solace from what it offers.
- May you always seek the truth to understand and advocate for those less fortunate.
- May you always remain curious and ask questions to deepen your perspective about life and the many topics that are of interest to you.
- May you always define your own success, and have the strength to assert that vision even in the face of others' judgment.
- May you always remember that no matter what you do, or don't do with your life, I will always love you.

Different Paths

The purpose of life is to discover your gift. The meaning of life is to give your gift away.

—David Viscott

These interviews offer a variety of perspectives on what it's like to take time off before, during, or after college.

Chris - The Bee Keeper

Chris attended high school at the Graham School in Columbus, Ohio where they stressed experiential learning and co-ops. He wanted to be a veterinarian and shadowed one who politely advised against this path. Before Chris graduated, he explored attending several of the big land grant schools like Cornell, but found a home at Warren Wilson College in Asheville, North Carolina, where he thought it was a better fit.

He'd been a bee keeper since age 12 and had an opportunity to continue his bee keeping on campus. He always had an interest in farming, so Patrick Ross, his supervisor on the school garden crew at Warren Wilson, suggested he attend the Biodynamic Conference in Red Boiling Springs, Tennessee. The conference would be held at Long Hungry Farms, owned by Jeff Poppen, (aka The Barefoot Farmer), a nationally known organic farmer and author. Ross knew Poppen and also secured funding for 10 of his students to attend.

Chris did an internship there later where he "learned about living with people of different lifestyles and a practical knowledge of farming." Poppen has welcomed more than 100 interns to his farm over the years.

Chris had completed two years of his bio chemistry major when he met AmeriCorps recruiters on campus. It seemed like a good match for him as one of his goals was to graduate from college with little debt. He took a leave of absence from school for a year and joined the National Civilian Community Corps (NCCC), where he provided disaster relief in Texas and supported other community services efforts in Arizona and Kansas. In addition to traveling, he learned how to participate in a team environment and on project-based assignments.

A year and a half later, he graduated from Warren Wilson with a chemistry degree and went back to Poppen's farm for another stint. He heard that farming is time-consuming and that if he wanted to see the world, he'd better do it now.

Chris went to Spain, where he made his way across the country living and working on farms including one in a small village on a mountaintop.

When he returned to the States, he went to work for a company that had 6,000 bee hives in Wisconsin and Florida. For a period of time, he traveled between the two states.

Today, at age 25, Chris has 60 hives of his own in five locations and works at an Amazon warehouse in Columbus. The job gives him money, healthcare, and the flexibility to pursue his goal of being a full-time bee keeper.

Throughout his journey, he says he's fortunate to have parents who have been "super supportive."

His only regret? That he didn't enter AmeriCorps right after high school.

Tara - The Explorer

She left her parents' home when she was 18 and got a job down the road in Athens, Georgia.

This event launched Tara on a journey of discovery, adventure, and enlightenment.

"I knew I would go to college, but I had a hard time—and still do—figuring out why I wanted to go." She was leery of taking on debt if the outcome was uncertain. "I knew it would have to be something I was passionate about and know that my money was going toward something I could use."

Tara was homeschooled for a couple of years, which allowed her to travel with her mother to ride horses at show arenas for money. She also attended a small high school in Monroe, Georgia, where her favorite class was horticulture. She liked the class, which was taught in the school's greenhouse, because she could "understand where things come from."

The end of school came with the stress of entrance testing and making decisions regarding where she would go to school, live, and work.

She found a cheap place to live in Athens, got a job as a waitress working 35 hours a week and entered community college to study communications with the goal of going into agriculture. After she graduated, she was still stressed out, unhappy, and wondering what to do next.

One day at the gym, she entered a happenstance moment when a friend told her about the National Outdoor Leadership School (NOLS)—a program that would be life-changing for her.

"He helped me get a scholarship and apply for loans. I had no idea what I had in store. I thought it would be camping for 80 days. I needed to get away from the place I had lived my whole life."

Some friends thought this move was curious. "If you don't stay on the path after high school, go straight to college and then grad school, you're considered very strange, probably like a wild one," Tara recalls.

They thought she was going away in the woods to find herself. That turned out to be true, but the nationally recognized program that has locations in six countries was more than camping; it taught her environmental ethics, technical outdoors skills, wilderness medicine, risk management and judgment, and leadership on extended wilderness expeditions and in traditional classrooms.

"I had great instructors. You have the opportunity to branch out and find something you love to do. You're allowed to come out of your box."

Participants stay together in groups of eight over the length of the program, which can create opportunities for plenty of conflict. This was a new skillset for her. "Usually, if you have conflict on the job or you make a mistake, you just run away. You don't have that opportunity there; you learn to adjust, learn to accept yourself. You grow with each other. It taught me to take and give feedback."

She learned about the quadrant of leadership styles and which style works best for her. "You look at everything differently. You look at things from the big picture in case you're missing something. I never had that before."

One of the climbing instructors taught her to be more assertive. Before NOLS, she said she felt embarrassed to ask questions about anything. He told her: "There are no questions you could ask that would ever make us not love you. Nothing is going to turn us against you."

She moved back to Georgia after completing the NOLS program, renewed and inspired. "I had a whole different mindset; I wasn't worried about getting married or having children or going back to school. I had this whole other set of dreams."

Creating art using welding had always been a strong interest of hers, so the new confident Tara emailed the owner of a welding shop who agreed to take her on as an apprentice. She was the only woman in the shop but that didn't deter her from asking questions to learn this new skill.

Agriculture had been a persistent theme in her life since high school so she decided to spend three months on a farm as an apprentice. Later, she served as the outreach coordinator for the Athens Farmers Market where she "...taught people about where their food comes from—young, old, diverse—that's where my passion is."

She realized that sustainability was a passion and found a job as a production manager for a small, local coffee roaster in Athens that minimizes waste and uses sustainable cups. "I want to live a sustainable life. It's more about mindful living."

These days, the self-described "mousey" student in high school waits for the next adventure. On a whim, she signed up to be a crew member on a sailboat. She received an email from the owner of the boat, an Englishman with a French partner, who said they were down a crew member and if she wanted to race on Lake Lanier, be at the dock at 5:30 that evening. "I was like: I got to go to this dock at 5:30." It was her first sailboat race and they invited her back the next week.

Tara's views on education have shifted drastically after her NOLS experience. "I've learned more from mentors in my life than I've learned from the classroom. It's great when you talk to someone who is passionate about what they do and education has helped them grow in that field."

And she no longer thinks you have to go to college to be successful. "I'm creating my own education."

Christian - The Traveler

"My parents wanted me to be happy," recounts Christian who was trying to decide what to do after graduating from the University School of Nashville (USN). It was always expected that he was going to college, but he didn't know if he wanted to go in the fall after graduation.

He applied to several schools and observed the frenzy of his classmates stressing over making the right choice and trying to get an edge in the process. "I was stressed, but some of my classmates were worse, especially the ones applying to the Ivy's." Some students told him he had to join certain clubs or organizations, because it would help on his applications. "I never was into that and don't think it helps that much anyway."

His parents are from Denmark and moved to the States when he was 11 years old. Before that, they lived in Australia for five years. Christian had traveled on business trips with his father to other countries and his mother who traveled frequently in the fashion industry.

During the summer of his high school junior year, his father casually mentioned the idea that Christian might move to Copenhagen after graduation to live by himself. It hadn't occurred to him, but after some consideration, he thought it might be "exciting." When he told his college-bound friends that he wasn't going to college right away, some couldn't believe it and thought it "was totally wrong."

At first, it sounded like an adventure. He was returning to the country where he'd been born and would explore what came next when he got there. "I didn't think of it as a gap year, I thought I was just moving to Copenhagen." His grandmother lived an hour from the city, but other than her, he didn't know anyone. "I am from there, but it was still a foreign country to me."

Christian had no gap year plan after he graduated from high school. His idea was simple: he would get a small apartment and get a job. But, he discovered that jobs were not easy to find, especially since he had no work experience.

After two months of biking from business to business (you don't need a car in Copenhagen), he landed a part-time job as a runner at a bar, moving kegs around at the back of the bar, washing dishes, and cleaning. Next, he got a full-time office job typing email addresses into a database eight hours a day; this was followed by a job at a fancy restaurant with what he describes as a "very demanding boss." "I had to learn to carry three plates at a time and I spilled wine on people all the time. It was stressing me out."

Things had not turned out like he had imagined; he had made no friends in the city and said he was starting to get depressed about the situation. Even his grandmother said he needed to make a change.

Christian's father offered a solution. He had set aside a small amount of money for each of the children to receive when they turned age 18, and they could do whatever they wanted with it. He suggested that Christian leave Copenhagen and travel until he started school in the fall.

He'd always enjoyed traveling with his dad on business trips to destinations like Laos, China, Hong Kong and Vietnam, so he left Copenhagen and flew to Berlin, then London, Prague, Hungary, Slovenia, Serbia, Bosnia, Italy, and Turkey. He stayed in hostels when he could and found cheap flights to keep expenses down.

In May and June, he went to Egypt, the West Bank, Israel, Jordon and Africa.

"I learned a lot about myself; I know myself better. In Copenhagen I had a lot of time to think." He said traveling gave him a sense of independence. When he decided to attend Reed College later that fall, he felt more independent than some of the freshmen he was around and found himself hanging out with older classmates.

The experience taught him some things that are important to him. "I don't know what the meaning of my life is, but I definitely know I want to travel as much as I can. I like learning how other people live. Maybe I'll get a job working for the U.N. one day."

Tiger - The Hands-On Learner

When Tiger received an "F" on a math test the end of his junior year in high school, it was a critical moment. He was frustrated that the grade wasn't a reflection of his knowledge, but rather a lack of motivation to focus on learning only to pass a test.

Tiger attended Wellesley High School, located in Wellesley, MA, known for its strong academics and push for students to attend the "best" colleges and universities when they graduated. He had worked hard his first two years to do well in school, but, by junior year, he had become disillusioned and disengaged. Tiger found the culture of the school too heavily focused on grades and on performing well on tests. He needed something different.

Luck was on his side. When he heard about a new program, *Evolutions*, starting at his school his senior year, Tiger applied, and was accepted. The hands-on, project-based, interdisciplinary learning approach was a perfect fit for him. He thrived as he engaged with other students in exploring the use and application of knowledge in their lives, their communities, and the world. *Evolutions* changed his life's trajectory.

Expected to go to college, Tiger joined the rest of his senior classmates who were applying to "safety" schools and "reach" schools. The process was stressful—not so much the decision to go, but where to apply. He ended up applying to 10 schools, was accepted into three, and ultimately decided to attend the University of Vermont (UVM) where he planned to study computer science.

A visit to campus for orientation, however, had him second-guessing his decision. He did not see himself at UVM for four years but felt committed to start in the fall since he had paid his deposit. He planned to transfer to another school once he completed his general education requirements.

An "a-ha" moment came when he realized that it did not make sense to start a school when he was already thinking of transferring. What could he do instead? A gap year. He had heard about "gap years" when he attended an information meeting during his junior year in high school. It made sense for him to take a year when he could be immersed into learning outside the classroom. *Evolutions* had laid the foundation for his interest in education reform; why not explore this during his year off?

Decision made and permission received from his mom and dad to delay starting college, Tiger researched gap year programs online related to education; a program called *City Year* captured his interest. It was an education non-profit headquartered in Boston that partnered with public schools in high-need communities across the US. Volunteers received a stipend for the year, so it was an affordable option for him.

Tiger applied and was accepted. He completed six weeks of training and was assigned to a team of five to serve at an elementary school in Hyde Park, a neighborhood in south Boston. To save money, Tiger lived at home and commuted to work. His primary role was to act as a tutor and mentor for 19 fifth graders. Throughout the year, Tiger received coaching and feedback on how to effectively mentor. At 18, he felt empowered as he worked alongside 22 and 23-year-old college graduates. The reasons they were volunteering with *City Year* varied, but most were using the time to figure out what was next since graduating.

With a clearer understanding of what he wanted from college, Tiger applied and was accepted to American University—a college known for student access to internships, in Washington, DC. He was interested in education policy, so he enrolled in an interdisciplinary major that combined communications, legal institutions, economics, and government. An internship during his second semester, however, ignited Tiger's interest in public service. He was hooked on the excitement and mission-driven work inherent in legislative work and its potential impact on society. He decided to switch majors to political science.

Tiger described his undergraduate experience as being "turbulent" but felt there was a thread tying it all together. The themes being: 1) experiential learning—going out and doing things opposed to just sitting in a classroom; 2) focusing on actual accomplishments and achievement versus measuring success by a grade; and 3) diving into something with his whole being and, if he failed, not to write it off as a loss.

Three years after volunteering with *City Year*, Tiger reflected on the continued impact of taking a gap year, "It was so dramatically different from what I thought I was going to do and from what everyone else was doing. It informed everything from that point on beginning with my freshman year at AU."

"Work ethic, motivation, all these big broad concepts of things that people try and tell students school is going to teach them, and it doesn't. That's really what a gap year gave me. I understand the value and importance of real-world experience that does not happen in a classroom lecture."

Maytal - The Sustainability Adventurer

Maytal thought after graduating from high school in Raleigh, North Carolina, that she would go to college, wind up in the arts, and maybe get a job at Sotheby's one day. But that was before she spent five months in Israel.

Her parents (her father was a chef, her mother, a sommelier) ran one of the first farm-to-table restaurants in the Southeast. "I was the 3-year-old handing out food samples at farmer's markets." Growing up in the South, she enjoyed being outdoors, hiking, and camping, and loved going to summer camp in Georgia.

Her parents hoped that after graduation Maytal would visit Israel where her dad grew up living and working in an agricultural community.

She wanted to travel internationally after high school and had explored the Carpe Diem Education program in East Africa because she wasn't sold on the idea of going to Israel. "I was hesitant, because I didn't want to do the regular touristy program." She thought if she were going to go, she wanted an experience that related to some of her interests. "I wanted something more authentic."

After Google searches on areas like "outdoors and camping," she discovered the Masa Israel Journey (masa means "journey" in Hebrew). The program is the leader in immersive international experiences in Israel for young adults, ages 18-30, and offers study, volunteer, and career development in their programs. Unfortunately, only a few programs fit her criteria.

Maytal wound up working for five months at the Hava Ve Adam Farm, an off-the-grid permaculture farm (the development of agricultural ecosystems intended to be sustainable, regenerative, and self-sufficient), in a zero-waste community. One of her jobs was working with a team on compost toilets where she learned that "waste does not exist."

She didn't realize it at the time, but the experience she now calls "life-changing" brought together several of her passions from growing up in North Carolina: the outdoors, farms, and food.

"Sustainability is now completely my passion." So much that she changed her major to environmental studies when she returned to the States. The student who sometimes struggled in the classroom had finally found a purpose. "Now, I know where I'm going."

This experience gave her confidence to try other agriculture adventures like WWOOFing (World-wide Opportunities on Organic Farms) for three weeks in Hawaii after her freshman year at the University of Colorado Boulder. After her sophomore year, she worked on a Trail Crew in Colorado maintaining and building trails and bridges for 10 weeks. She lived in a tent from June to August and decided to continue this arrangement until December to avoid the pandemic as much as possible.

Maytal was living in Israel when she received the devastating news that her father had committed suicide. Shell-shocked, she struggled to make sense of the tragedy and how she would move forward. Before his death, she had planned to participate in the Carpe Diem program in East Africa.

"At the time it was important for me to continue with my plans. I didn't want my dad's death to define my life or my gap year. He was excited for me to have this experience and so it was important for me to continue on my path." She and one of her brothers later hiked a marathon in his memory with donations going to The Quell Foundation, a non-profit that raises awareness about mental health issues.

She chose East Africa, because "I wanted to travel to the most off the beaten path, scariest remote place I could find" so she wouldn't feel intimidated traveling anywhere on her own. Communication systems were challenging in the remote areas, so it was hard for her to share thoughts of grieving with her family.

Once she got anchored in the new experience, she discovered that every day and every location was different. In Tanzania she took language classes in Swahili; in Zanzibar she worked in a natural herbal spa.

She learned about conservation and witnessed sometimes simple solutions to complex problems. Farmers in Tanzania, outside of Ruaha National Park, were killing elephants, because they were destroying their crops. Maytal was part of a group that constructed bee hive fences that created loud buzzing sounds in the elephant's large ears when they got close. Problem solved. Farmers could also make money from selling the honey.

Carpe Diem establishes relationships with the communities where they have programs so students are living and working within the culture. The experience was humbling. "I realize how I lucky and privileged I am to be in school. Something like 6% of world population goes to a university."

Her agriculture and sustainability experiences in Israel, East Africa and in the United States have positioned her for what's next. "I see myself as a life-long adventurer, constantly looking for my next adventure. It's who I am." She said that after graduation, she may join the Peace Corps or work for Carpe Diem.

She has advice for students considering gap years or time away from school. "Don't be afraid to do the absolute scariest thing. It sets you up for really. Gap years can prepare you for that. A gap year gave me the opportunity to take my degree seriously."

Am I Too Late?

Your Turn

Steps:

1. Gather resources to make informed decisions

2. Have honest discussions with your learner about next steps

3. Ensure all players are on board

4. Create a draft of a plan

5. Adjust your plan as needed and have regular check ins about how your young adult is doing mentally, physically, and emotionally

6. Don't be discouraged when things change

7. Remember what you are trying to accomplish

8. Know that all learning is valuable and will continue throughout your child's lifetime

9. There is strength in numbers—join groups with other parents who will support you and your learner

Remember that it's never "too late."

Am I Too Late?

In Gratitude

This book would not be possible if Jim Bellar had not emailed me two years ago and offered to collaborate with me on this project. He knew Mackenzie's story and believed it was an important one to share with families engaged in the high school to college transition. His encouragement was just what I needed to return to the book project I had started in Spring 2017 but had put aside after suffering a head injury that summer. My recovery took over a year and because I found that I had lost my ability to focus, I stopped writing. I now have a greater appreciation for others who have suffered from head injuries or other cognitive challenges.

I am glad to share that, with a lot of work, I have fully recovered and am enjoying good health for which I am grateful. Jim and I began our book collaboration around the time that COVID-19 was making an appearance in the US last year. Like many, I hunkered at home during the pandemic, and as a result, had lots of time to think and write. With Jim's continued friendship, guidance, and contributions to the writing process along with his positivity and sense of humor, we made monthly progress toward our goal. Working with Jim has been my favorite part of this book project and I will be forever indebted to him for his "nudge." I owe Kathy Bellar, his wife, a huge "thank you" for giving him time to work on this book while he was finishing his Southern Gothic novel, *The Deal*, and working on other writing projects.

As you might be able to ascertain from reading this book, I am fortunate to have strong family support which made this book possible. I would like to thank my brother Jeff Funk and sister-in-law Agnes Weber for allowing me to use their Sisters, OR home as my writing studio. They have always been champions of Mike, the "boys", and me as we have made a number of life transitions. My sister and brother-in-law Melodie and Steve Henderson are also important individuals to recognize for the support they have given to me and on-going interest in the subject. They live in the Boston area where the focus on college-prep has created a mental health epidemic for youth. My sister and brother-in-law Carla and

Tom Wittum are also owed a huge debt of gratitude. Mackenzie and Stuart spent many summers visiting them in Ohio developing close relationships with their children Kelsi, Chris, and Renna. Their generosity of opening their home for many years as a de facto summer camp made it possible for me to work full-time and Mike complete his PhD. My brother Dan Funk, an author in his own right, has provided much support over the years, including saying "yes" when we asked if we could come and stay in Australia for Mike's walkabout. I have constantly been cheered on by him and Alli Hossack, his wife, throughout this writing journey. My "sister" Mary Jo Kleeman has always supported me with her generosity during many years when finances were tight. From providing housing while Mackenzie worked at the ski area to helping buy plane tickets for us to return to Colorado to spend time with family, she has continued to play an integral role in my life. I also want to thank my mother-in-law Carolyn Myers whose strength and faith have inspired me to never give up.

Other individuals that I would like to thank include Judie Betts, my artist friend in Navarre Beach, who models that you can do anything at any age; my former naturopath Stephanie Farrell, who urged me to use my "voice" to help other parents like herself worried about their children's anxiety and pressure to "do" well at school; my friends Jenny Huq and Kara Bingham, international and experiential education professionals, who have shared their expertise with me; my former Vandy colleague and friend Nina Warnke, who has continued to offer support and insight into the issues of young adults; my Massage Therapist Claire Darling whose healing touch assisted my recovery and whose on-going cheerleading has helped tremendously during this writing journey; my friends Joy Armstrong, Lynn Rhodes, and Tiana Julian for always believing in me.

A special shout out to all the beta readers who agreed to read this book— their feedback was invaluable; to all those who we interviewed for this book including Christian Hahnemann, Chris Cree, Maytal Agasi, Tiger Mar, Tara Watkins, Tom Van Winkle, and Cristin Viebranz—their generosity and willingness to share their perspective helped provide important context on different topics; my coach and friend Stephanie Brodtrick who has continued to challenge and support me professionally and personally over the years; Peter and Precious Inampasa whose generosity and kindness toward Mackenzie and our family over the years will never be forgotten; my niece Kelsi who helped me take needed breaks through Zoom yoga over the past year; and my long-time friend

Carol Webster for the many hours she spent in proofing and editing copy for the book.

I am also grateful to the following champions of gap years and education reform whose work have been an inspiration to me—Chris Unger, Rae Nelson, Holly Bull, and the Gap Year Association and its members.

Finally, I would like to express my gratitude to my mom, Jody Funk, who has always believed and encouraged me without judgment, and my dad Carl Funk—though he is no longer with us—is the voice in my head saying, "there is no such thing as try, just do."

For my husband Mike Myers, I would not have been able to complete this project without his support. The journey to publish has been made easier with the expertise that he brought to writing, editing, and the creative process. His love and friendship have continued to lift me up when times have been challenging. I am grateful for my son Stuart Myers who continues to inspire me with his grit and courage and his willingness to hug his Mom when she needs one.

And last, but not least, I want to thank Mackenzie Myers for saying "yes" to sharing his story. I am humbled by the faith that he placed in me and his willingness to be vulnerable in order to help others in their journey navigating the high school to college transition.

Keep Learning,

Cindy Funk

Am I Too Late?

About the Authors

Cindy Funk is a higher education consultant, career and life coach, and author currently living in Portland, Oregon. She has over twenty years professional experience working in career services at public and private institutions including Vanderbilt University, Colorado College, Regis University, the University of Colorado at Colorado Springs, and Portland State University. Her entrepreneurial ventures include launching a gourmet popcorn manufacturing operation and converting a fitness center into a residential property featured on HGTV. She is the parent of two college-age sons who both chose to take a gap year before making the transition to college.

Jim Bellar is an author, musician and consultant based in the Nashville area. After high school, he dropped out of college after one semester, which sent him on a journey that included time as a combat infantry soldier, a janitor, heating and air conditioning installer, and a reporter before he received a bachelor's degree in his late twenties. He has held management and leadership positions in workforce development and at Vanderbilt University and has been a presenter at national and international career development conferences.

Notes

[1] Gardner, David Pierpont. *A Nation at Risk: the Imperative for Educational Reform: A Report to the Nation and the Secretary of Education*. The National Commission on Excellence in Education, 1983.

[2] Lino, Mark, et al. *Expenditures on Children by Families, 2015*. Miscellaneous Publication No. 1528-2015. U.S. Department of Agriculture, Center for Nutrition Policy and Promotion, 2017.

[3] "What Is Montessori Education?" American Montessori Society, amshq.org/About-Montessori/What-Is-Montessori.

[4] Busteed, Brandon. "What's The Purpose Of College?" *Forbes*, 10 Apr. 2019, www.forbes.com/sites/brandonbusteed/2019/04/10/whats-the-purpose-of-college/.

[5] "When it comes to paying for college, career school, or graduate school, federal student loans can offer several advantages over private student loans." *Federal Student Aid An Office of the U.S. Department of Education*. www.studentaid.gov/understand-aid/types/loans.

[6] Friedman, Zack. "Student Loan Debt Statistics In 2020: A Record $1.6 Trillion." *Forbes*, 3 Feb. 2020, www.forbes.com/sites/zackfriedman/ 2020/02/03/student-loan-debt-statistics/.

[7] Friedman, Zack. "Wait, Parents Owe $100 Billion Of Student Loans?" *Forbes*, 24 Feb. 2020, www.forbes.com/sites/zackfriedman/ 2020/02/24/refinance-parent-plus-loans/.

[8] Kelsey, Brenda. "Helping Students Choose a Major." *Student Research Foundation*, 10 Sep. 2018, www.studentresearchfoundation.org/blog/ helping-students-choose-a-major/.

9 Marcus, Jon. "Changing majors is adding time and tuition to the high cost of college." *The Hechinger Report*, 7 Dec. 2018, hechingerreport.org/switching-majors-is-adding-time-and-tuition-to-the-already-high-cost-of-college/.

10 Fain, Paul. "Second Thoughts About Higher Education Decisions." I*nside Higher Ed*, 1 Jun. 2017, www.insidehighered.com/news/2017/06/01/survey-finds-regrets-among-most-former-college-students-belief-quality-their.

11 Taylor, Ben."21 Wildly Successful CEOs With Liberal Arts Degrees." *Business 2 Community*, 4 Aug. 2015, www.business2community.com/leadership/21-wildly-successful-ceos-with-liberal-arts-degrees-01293809.

12 Fain, Paul. "Philosophy Degrees and Sales Jobs." *Inside Higher Ed*, 2 Aug. 2019, www.insidehighered.com/news/2019/08/02/new-data-track-graduates-six-popular-majors-through-their-first-three-jobs.

13 Selingo, Jeffrey. "Why Do so Many Students Drop out of College? And What Can Be Done about It?" *The Washington Post*, 8 Jun. 2018, www.washingtonpost.com/news/grade-point/wp/2018/06/08/why-do-so-many-students-drop-out-of-college-and-what-can-be-done-about-it/.

14 Huffman, Mark. "Despite low unemployment, many college grads are out of work." *Consumer Affairs*, 18 Jun. 2018, www.consumeraffairs.com/news/despite-low-unemployment-many-college-grads-are-out-of-work-061818.html.

15 Wilkie, Dana. "Employers Say Students Aren't Learning Soft Skills in College." *SHRM*, 28 Feb. 2020, www.shrm.org/resourcesandtools/hr-topics/employee-relations/pages/employers-say-students-arent-learning-soft-skills-in-college.aspx.

16 Friedman, Zack. "50% Of Millennials Are Moving Back Home With Their Parents." *Forbes*, 6 Jun. 2019, www.forbes.com/sites/zackfriedman/2019/06/06/millennials-move-back-home-college/.

17 Fry, Richard, et al. "A majority of young adults in the U.S. live with their parents for the first time since the Great Depression." *Fact Tank: News in Numbers,* Pew Research Center, 4 Sept. 2020, www.pewresearch.org/fact-tank/2020/09/04/a-majority-of-young-adults-in-the-u-s-live-with-their-parents-for-the-first-time-since-the-great-depression/.

18 Fadulu, Lola. "Why aren't college students using career services." *The Atlantic* 20, 2018.

19 Fain, Paul. "Philosophy Degrees and Sales Jobs." *Inside Higher Ed*, 2 Aug. 2019, www.insidehighered.com/news/2019/08/02/new-data-track-graduates-six-popular-majors-through-their-first-three-jobs.

20 Long, Heather. "The new normal: 4 job changes by the time you're 32." *CNN Business*, 12 Apr. 2016, money.cnn.com/2016/04/12/news/economy/millennials-change-jobs-frequently/index.html.

21 Mazhukhina, Karina. "Will your job be around in 2030? Nearly 40% won't, report says." *Komo News*, 2 Aug. 2019, komonews.com/news/local/will-your-job-be-around-in-2030-nearly-40-wont-report-says.

22 Ray Mauer, "Why Are Workers Quitting Their Jobs in Record Numbers?." *SHRM, 12 Dec. 2018,* www.shrm.org/resourcesandtools/hr-topics/talent-acquisition/pages/workers-are-quitting-jobs-record-numbers.aspx.

23 Unger, Chris. "A Revolution in Education." Audio blog post. *A REVOLUTION IN EDUCATION*, www.arevolutionineducation.org/.

24 Davidson, Cathy N. *The New Education: How to Revolutionize the University to Prepare Students for a World in Flux.* Basic Books, 2017.

25 "Thinking of College in Europe?" *Beyond the States*, 21 Apr. 2021, beyondthestates.com/.

26 Viemont, Jennifer. *College beyond the States: European Schools That Will Change Your Life without Breaking the Bank.* Global Ed Press, 2018.

27 University School of Nashville, www.usn.org/.

28 "Programs." *Programs | Duke TIP*, tip.duke.edu/programs.

29 "The ACT Test for Students | ACT." www.actstudent.org/.

30 "The SAT | College Board." collegereadiness.collegeboard.org/sat.

31 Munger, Katy. "Duke TIP Recognizes Seventh Graders Nationwide for Their Exceptional Academic Abilities." *Duke Tip*, 20 Apr. 2016, tip.duke.edu/about/news/duke-tip-recognizes-seventh-graders-nationwide-their-exceptional-academic-abilities.

32 *National Merit Scholarship Qualifications*, www.studypoint.com/ed/
national-merit-scholarship-qualifications/.

33 Karlgaard, Rich. *Late bloomers: The power of patience in a world
obsessed with early achievement.* Currency, 2019.

34 "Discover AP." *Advanced Placement (AP) – The College Board*,
ap.collegeboard.org/.

35 Zhou, Amanda. "Students are taking AP exams, but researchers don't
know if that helps them." *Chalkbeat*, 3 Aug. 2018, chalkbeat.org/posts/
us/2018/08/03/more-students-are-taking-ap-exams-but-researchers-
dont-know-if-that-helps-them/.

36 Kallick, Bena, and Giselle O. Martin-Kniep. "Establishing a three-way
relationship in service of deeper learning." ASCD in Service, 15 Sept.
2020, inservice.ascd.org/establishing-a-three-way-relationship-in-
service-of-deeper-learning/

37 *The Myers & Briggs Foundation - MBTI Basics*,
www.myersbriggs.org/my-mbti-personality-type/mbti-basics/.

38 Moody, Josh. "What to Know About Early Action, Early Decision in
College." *US News and World Report*, 20 Mar. 2020, www.usnews.com/
education/best-colleges/articles/what-to-know-about-early-action-early-
decision-in-college-admissions.

39 "Getting into College | What to Do if You're Waitlisted - BigFuture."
College Board, bigfuture.collegeboard.org/get-in/making-a-decision/
what-to-do-if-youre-wait-listed.

40 Whistle, Wesley. "The Varsity Blues College Admissions Scandal
Continues." *Forbes*, 3 Sept. 2020, www.forbes.com/sites/wesleywhistle/
2020/09/03/the-varsity-blues-college-admissions-scandal-continues/.

41 Kastner, Laura Scribner, et al. *The launching years: Strategies for
parenting from senior year to college life.* Harmony, 2002.

42 Arnett, Jeffrey Jensen. *Emerging adulthood: The winding road from
the late teens through the twenties.* Oxford University Press, 2014.

43 Sizer, Nancy Faust. "Reclaiming Senior Year." *National Association of
Independent Schools,* Winter 2003, www.nais.org/magazine/
independent-school/winter-2003/reclaiming-senior-year/.

44 Horn, Michael B., and Bob Moesta. *Choosing college: How to make better learning decisions throughout your life*. John Wiley & Sons, 2019.

45 Dintersmith, Ted. *What School Could Be Insights and Inspiration from Teachers across America*. Princeton University Press, 2018.

46 "Mastery Transcript Consortium." https://mastery.org.

47 Parks, Sharon Daloz. *Big questions, worthy dreams: Mentoring emerging adults in their search for meaning, purpose, and faith*. John Wiley & Sons, 2011.

48 Deresiewicz, William. *Excellent sheep: The miseducation of the American elite and the way to a meaningful life*. Simon and Schuster, 2015.

49 Seaman, Barrett. *Binge: What your college student won't tell you*. John Wiley & Sons, 2005.

50 Dintersmith, Ted. *What school could be: Insights and inspiration from teachers across America*. Princeton University Press, 2018.

51 "What Is a Gap Year." *Gap Year Association*, www.gapyearassociation.org/educators.php.

52 Murchison, Colin, et al. "USA Gap Year Fairs." *Go Overseas*, 26 Apr. 2021, www.gooverseas.com/gap-year/usa-fairs.

53 Haigler, Karl, and Rae Nelson. *The gap-year advantage: Helping your child benefit from time off before or during college*. Macmillan, 2005.

54 White, Kristin M. *The complete guide to the gap year: the best things to do between high school and college*. John Wiley & Sons, 2009.

55 Griffiths, Susan. *Your Gap Year. The Most Comprehensive Guide to an Exciting and Fulfilling Gap Year*. Crimson Publishing, 2012.

56 "Gap Year Data & Benefits." *Gap Year Association*." www.gapyearassociation.org/data-benefits.php.

57 O'Shea, Joseph. *Gap year: How delaying college changes people in ways the world needs*. JHU Press, 2014.

58 "Gap Year Research Consortium at Colorado College." sites.coloradocollege.edu/gapyearresearchconsortium/.

59 NACE staff. "The Four Career Competencies Employers Value Most." *National Association of College and Employers*, 29 Mar. 2019, www.naceweb.org/career-readiness/competencies/the-four-career-competencies-employers-value-most/.

60 Abel, Jaison R., and Richard Deitz. "Delaying College During the Pandemic Can Be Costly." *Liberty Street Economics*, libertystreeteconomics.newyorkfed.org/2020/07/delaying-college-during-the-pandemic-can-be-costly.html.

61 Horn, Michael B. "New York Fed Researchers Wrong About Gap Years." *Forbes*, 10 Aug. 2020, www.forbes.com/sites/michaelhorn/2020/08/11/new-york-fed-researchers-wrong-about-gap-years/.

62 Horn, Michael B. "New York Fed Researchers Wrong About Gap Years." *Forbes*, 10 Aug. 2020, www.forbes.com/sites/michaelhorn/2020/08/11/new-york-fed-researchers-wrong-about-gap-years/.

63 McRoberts, Sam. "Here's What Science Says You Should Do to Achieve Greater Success." *Entrepreneur*, Entrepreneur, 29 Dec. 2017, www.entrepreneur.com/article/305985.

64 Ware, Bronnie. *The Top Five Regrets of the Dying: a Life Transformed by the Dearly Departing*. Hay House Australia, 2019.

65 McConaughey, Matthew. *Greenlights*. Crown, 2020.

66 Wheatley, Margaret J., and Deborah Frieze. *Walk out walk on: A learning journey into communities daring to live the future now*. Berrett-Koehler Publishers, 2011.

67 *AmeriCorps*, 13 May 2021, americorps.gov/.

68 Louv, Richard. *Last Child in the Woods: Saving Our Children from Nature-Deficit Disorder*. Atlantic Books, 2013.

69 "About NOLS." *NOLS*, www.nols.edu/en/about/about/.

70 Kanengieter, John, and Aparna Rajagopal-Durbin. "Wilderness Leadership-on the Job." *Harvard Business Review*, 1 Aug. 2014, hbr.org/2012/04/wilderness-leadership-on-the-job.

71 Busteed, Brandon. "Why Aren't Graduates Ready For Work? They're The Least Working Generation In U.S. History." *Forbes*, 29 Mar. 2019, www.forbes.com/sites/brandonbusteed/2019/03/29/why-arent-graduates-ready-for-work-theyre-the-least-working-generation-in-us-history/.

72 Gallup, Inc. "What Is the Difference between a Talent and a Strength?" *Gallup.com*, Gallup, 23 Jan. 2012, www.strengthsquest.com/help/general/143096/difference-talent-strength.aspx.

73 Clifton, Donald O., et al. *StrengthsQuest: Discover and Develop Your Strengths in Academics, Career, and Beyond.* Gallup Press, 2006.

74 *The Government of The Kingdom of Eswatini*, www.gov.sz/index.php.

75 Maathai, Wangari. *The challenge for Africa: A new vision.* Random House, 2009.

76 *Waterford Kamhlaba United World College Southern Africa - (WKUWCSA)*, www.waterford.sz/.

77 Watts, D. J. *Six Degrees: the Science of a Connected Age.* W.W. Norton & Company, 2003.

78 Parry, Danaan. *Essene Book of Days*. Earthstewards Network Publications, 2001.

79 Cacpr0. *Appulachian Trail Conservancy*, appalachiantrail.org/.

80 Bruffey, Daniel. "Thru-Hiking." *Appalachian Trail Conservancy*, appalachiantrail.org/explore/hike-the-a-t/thru-hiking/.

81 Bidgood, J., and Richard Perez-Pena. "Geraldine Largay's Wrong Turn: Death on the Appalachian Trail." *New York Times*, 26 May 2016, www.nytimes.com/2016/05/27/us/missing-hiker-geraldine-largay-appalachian-trail-maine.html.

82 "Paul's Boots – Follow the Story #PaulWalksOn – REI Blog." *REI Co-Op Journal*, www.rei.com/blog/paulsboots/story.

83 "The Blog of Williams-Mystic." williamsmystic.wordpress.com

84 Kallfelz, Laura. "World Wide Opportunities on Organic Farms." *WWOOF*, 13 Oct. 2020, www.wwoof.net/.

[85] *NOAA Hollings Undergraduate Scholarship*, www.noaa.gov/office-education/hollings-scholarship.

[86] "13 Symptoms and Signs of Lyne Disease." *Healthline*, 3 Aug. 2020, www.healthline.com/health/lyme-disease-symptoms.

[87] "Transmission." *Centers for Disease Control and Prevention*, Centers for Disease Control and Prevention, 29 Jan. 2020, www.cdc.gov/lyme/transmission/index.html.

[88] LitCharts. "Ulysses Summary & Analysis by Alfred Lord Tennyson." *LitCharts*, www.litcharts.com/poetry/alfred-lord-tennyson/ulysses.

[89] Holladay, J. Douglas. *Rethinking Success: Eight Essential Practices for Finding Meaning in Work and Life.* HarperCollins Publishers, 2020.

[90] "Competencies Overview." *SHRM CERTIFICATION*, 19 Mar. 2021, www.shrm.org/certification/about/body-of-competency-and-knowledge/Pages/Competencies-Overview.aspx.

[91] "Top 11 Skills Employers Look for in Candidates." *Indeed Career Guide*, www.indeed.com/career-advice/resumes-cover-letters/skills-employers-look-for.

[92] Pilgrim, Kristyn. "Perceptions of Gap Years Amid the Pandemic." *College Finance*, 30 Jul. 2020, collegefinance.com/blog/perceptions-of-gap-years-amid-the-pandemic

[93] Brand, Dionne. "Dionne Brand: On Narrative, Reckoning and the Calculus of Living and Dying." *Thestar.com*, 4 July 2020, www.thestar.com/entertainment/books/2020/07/04/dionne-brand-on-narrative-reckoning-and-the-calculus-of-living-and-dying.html.

[94] paperson, la. *A Third University is Possible.* University of Minnesota Press, 2017.

[95] Harney, Stefano, and Fred Moten. "The Undercommons: Fugitive Planning and Black Study." *Amazon*, Minor Compositions, 2013, www.amazon.com/Undercommons-Fugitive-Planning-Black-Study/dp/1570272670.

[96] Weise, Michelle. *Long Life Learning. Preparing for Jobs That Don't Even Exist Yet.* Wiley, 2020.

97 *Wayfinding Academy,* www.wayfindingacademy.org.

98 Obama, Michelle. *Becoming.* Crown Publishing Group (NY), 2018.

Made in the USA
Columbia, SC
27 June 2021

41055874R10153